Disarming the Darkness

GROWINGDEEPER

Disarming *the* Darkness

A Guide to Spiritual Warfare

Foreword by Eugene Peterson

Calvin Miller

ZondervanPublishingHouse
Grand Rapids, Michigan

A Division of HarperCollins*Publishers*

Disarming the Darkness
Copyright © 1998 by Calvin Miller

Requests for information should be addressed to:

≝ ZondervanPublishingHouse
Grand Rapids, Michigan 49530

Library of Congress Cataloging-in-Publication Data

Miller, Calvin.
    Disarming the darkness : a guide to spiritual warfare / Calvin Miller.
      p. cm.
    Includes bibliographical references.
    ISBN: 0-310-20196-9
    1. Spiritual Warfare.   2. Devil.   I. Title.
BV4509.5.M55   1998
235'.4—DC20   96–44160
                                                       CIP

This edition printed on acid-free paper and meets the American National
Standards Institute Z39.48 standard.

Published in association with the literary agency of Alive Communications, Inc.,
1465 Kelly Johnson Blvd., Suite 320, Colorado Springs, CO 80920.

Interior design by Sue Koppenol

Printed in the United States of America

---

98 99 00 01 02 03 04 /❖ DC/ 10 9 8 7 6 5 4 3 2 1

CONTENTS

Foreword by Eugene H. Peterson 7

Introduction 14

Part One: Understanding Spiritual Conflict

1. Enemy-Occupied Territory 17

2. The Fury of Angels 33

3. The Rumor of Victory 64

Part Two: Naming the Powers

4. Mammon: The Money Demon 91

5. Astarte: The Demon of Illicit Sexuality . . . 114

6. Beelzebub: The Demon of Power 135

Notes 157

FOREWORD
BY EUGENE H. PETERSON

A favorite story in our home as our children were growing up was of John Muir at the top of the Douglas fir in the storm.* Whenever we were assaulted by thunder and lightning, rain sluicing out of the sky, and the five of us, parents and three children, huddled together on the porch enjoying the dangerous fireworks from our safe ringside seat, one of the kids would say, "Tell us the John Muir story, Daddy!" And I'd tell it again.

In the last half of the nineteenth century, John Muir was our most intrepid and worshipful explorer of the western extremities of our North American continent. For decades he tramped up and down through our God-created wonders, from the California Sierras to the Alaskan glaciers, observing, reporting, praising, and experiencing—entering into whatever he found with childlike delight and mature reverence.

At one period during this time (the year was 1874) Muir visited a friend who had a cabin, snug in a valley of one of the tributaries of the Yuba River in the Sierra Mountains—a place from which to venture into the wilderness and then return for a comforting cup of tea.

One December day a storm moved in from the Pacific—a fierce storm, that bent the junipers and pines, the madronas and fir trees as if they were so many blades

---

*Edwin Way Teale, ed. *The Wilderness World of John Muir* (Boston: Houghton Mifflin, 1954), 181–90.

of grass. It was for just such times this cabin had been built: cozy protection from the harsh elements. We easily imagine Muir and his host safe and secure in his tightly caulked cabin, a fire blazing against the cruel assault of the elements, wrapped in sheepskins, Muir meditatively rendering the wildness into his elegant prose. But our imaginations, not trained to cope with Muir, betray us. For Muir, instead of retreating to the coziness of the cabin, pulling the door tight, and throwing another stick of wood on the fire, strode *out* of the cabin into the storm, climbed a high ridge, picked a giant Douglas fir as the best perch for experiencing the kaleidoscope of color and sound, scent and motion, scrambled his way to the top, and rode out the storm, lashed by the wind, holding on for dear life, relishing *Weather:* taking it all in—its rich sensuality, its primal energy.

<hr>

Throughout its many retellings, the story of John Muir, storm-whipped at the top of the Douglas fir in the Yuba River valley, gradually took shape as a kind of icon of Christian spirituality for our family. The icon has been in place ever since as a standing rebuke against becoming a mere spectator to life, preferring creature comforts to Creator confrontations.

For spirituality has to do with life, *lived* life. For Christians, "spirituality" is derived (always and exclusively) from Spirit, God's Holy Spirit. And "spirit," in the biblical languages of Hebrew and Greek, is the word "wind," or "breeze," or "breath"—an invisibility that has visible effects.

This is the Wind/Spirit that created all the life we both see and can't see (Genesis 1:2); that created the life of Jesus (Luke 1:35 and 3:22); that created a church of worshiping men and women (Acts 2:2–4); that creates each Christian (Romans 8:11). There is no accounting for life, any life, except by means of this Wind/Spirit:

> *Thou sendest forth thy spirit [breath/wind],*
> *   they are created:*
> *and thou renewest the face of the earth.*
> *(Psalm 104:30 KJV)*

There is clearly far more to Spirit-created living than can be detected by blood pressure and pulse rate. All the "vital signs" of botany, biology, and physiology combined hardly begin to account for life; if it doesn't also extend into matters far more complex than our circulatory and respiratory systems—namely, matters of joy and love, faith and hope, truth and beauty, meaning and value—there is simply not enough there to qualify as "life" for the common run of human beings on this planet earth. Most of us may not be able to define "spirituality" in a satisfactory way, but few of us fail to recognize its presence or absence. And to feel ourselves enhanced by its presence and diminished by its absence. Life, life, and more life—it's our deepest hunger and thirst.

But that doesn't always translate into Spirit, Spirit, and more Spirit in the conduct of our lives. Spirit, *Holy* Spirit, in Christian terminology, is God's life in our lives, God living in us and thereby making us participants in the extravagant prodigality of life, visible and invisible, that is Spirit-created.

We humans, somewhere along the way, seem to have picked up the bad habit of trying to get life on our terms, without all the bother of God, the Spirit of Life. We keep trying to be our own gods; and we keep making a sorry mess of it. Worse, the word has gotten around in recent years that "spirituality" itself might be a way of getting a more intense life without having to deal with God—spirituality as a kind of intuitive bypass around the inconvenience of repentance and sacrifice and putting ourselves at risk by following Jesus in the way of the cross, the very way Jesus plainly told was the only way to the "abundant life" that he had come to bless us with.

The generic name for this way of going about things—trying to put together a life of meaning and security out of God-sanctioned stories and routines, salted with weekends of diversion and occasional erotic interludes, without dealing firsthand, believingly and obediently, with God—is "religion." It is not, of course, a life without God, but the God who is there tends to be mostly background and resource—a Quality or Being that provides the ideas and energy that I take charge of and arrange and use as I see fit. We all of us do it, more or less.

The word "religion," following one possible etymology (not all agree on this), comes from the Latin, *religere*, "to bind up, or tie up, again." The picture that comes to my mind is of myself, having spent years "getting it all together," strolling through John Muir's Yuba River valley, enjoying the country, whistling in self-satisfaction, carrying my "life" bundled in a neat package—memories and morals, goals and diversions, prayers and devotion all sorted and tied together. And then the storm comes, fierce and sudden, a gust tears my packaged life from my arms and scatters the items every which way, all over the valley, all through the forest.

What do I then do? Do I run helter-skelter through the trees, crawl through the brush, frantically trying to recover all the pieces of my life, desperately enlisting the help of passersby and calling in the experts, searching for and retrieving and putting back together again (rebinding!) whatever I can salvage of my life, and then hiding out in the warm and secure cabin until the storm blows over? Or do I follow John Muir to the exposed ridge and the top of the Douglas fir, and open myself to the Weather, not wanting to miss a detail of this invasion of Life into my life, ready at the drop of a hat to lose my life to save it (Mark 8:35)?

For me, the life of religion (cautious and anxious, holding things together as best I can so that my life will make sense and, hopefully, please God), and the life of spirituality (a passion for life and a willingness to risk identity and security in following Jesus, no matter what) contrast in these two scenarios. There is no question regarding what I want: I want to be out in the Weather! But far more often than not I find myself crawling around on the ground, gathering up the pieces of my life and tying them together again in a secure bundle, safe from the effects of the Weather. Actually, the two ways of life can coexist; there is, after all, a place for steady and responsible routine—John Muir, after all, didn't spend all his time at the top of the Douglas fir; he spent most of his time on the valley floor. He also had a cabin that he had built with his own hands in which he received guests and prepared meals for them. But if there is no readiness to respond to the living God, who moves when and how and where he chooses, it isn't much of a life—the *livingness* soon leaks out of it.

౭ుడ౨

We cannot, of course, command Weather. It is there; it happens. There is no question of managing or directing it. There is no recipe for concocting "spirituality" any more than there is a chemical formula for creating "life." As Jesus most famously put it to that expert on the religious life, Nicodemus, "You know well enough how the wind blows this way and that. You hear it rustling through the trees, but you have no idea where it comes from or where it's headed next. That's the way it is with everyone 'born from above' by the wind of God, the Spirit of God" (John 3:8 THE MESSAGE).

The best we can do is to cultivate awareness, alertness, so that when the Wind blows we are *there*, ready to step into it—or not: when the absurd command comes to distribute the meager five loaves and two fish to the crowd we are ready to obey—or not; when direction is given to wait with the 120 for the promise, we are ready to wait—or not; when the invitation comes to "take . . . eat . . . drink," we are ready to come to the supper—or not.

∽⚬⚬∽

The books in this series, *Growing Deeper*, are what some of my friends and I do to stay alert and aware as we wait for the Wind to blow whether in furious storm or cooling breeze or gentle breathing—intending to cultivate and maintain a receptive readiness to the Spirit who brings us Life. They are not books *about* spirituality; they are simply accounts of what we do to stay awake to the Coming. There is nothing novel in any of them; our intent is to report what Christians have commonly done to stay present to the Spirit: we pray (Wangerin), preach and teach (Miller), meditate on the soul (Shaw), reflect on our checkered experiences with God's people (Yancey), and nurture Jesus-friends (Peterson).

Our shared conviction is that most of us in this "information age" have adequate access to facts; but in regards to *Life* (*Spirit*-formed spirituality), witness and motivation are always welcome.

Eugene H. Peterson
James Houston Professor of Spiritual Theology
Regent College
Vancouver, B.C., Canada

INTRODUCTION

The vast interest in the subject of spiritual warfare caused me to shrink from ever beginning to write this book. Several factors made me wary. First, scholars like Walter Wink and Clint Arnold and Sid Paige have long dedicated their scholarship to understanding the subject. Indeed, their fine research is often cited in this book as welcome sources of light in my own weaker understanding. With the light of their wisdom, I at last took up my pen in the hope of writing a simpler, if less scholarly, definition.

A work of this size must, of course, be introductory. I have not tried to be exhaustive, only thorough. So, much of the book includes my own experiences with the demonic as I have seen its influence on the lives of friends and acquaintances. In most cases I have changed the names to protect their privacy. I have written with a most important and elementary goal: I would like for you, my reader, to gain enough insight into the issue of spiritual warfare that you are neither afraid of nor overwhelmed by the subject.

As in all my books I have one key desire: I want Christ to be exalted and his Lordship to be the bond that makes my writing and your reading the mutual service we both give to him.

Calvin Miller
Southwestern Baptist Theological Seminary
Ft. Worth, Texas
September 1996

One

UNDERSTANDING SPIRITUAL CONFLICT

1

ENEMY-OCCUPIED TERRITORY

I know where you live—where Satan has his throne.

REVELATION 2:13

In 1974 my views of the occult were forever forged. Why 1974? Because in the mid-seventies, our culture became immersed in a cultural and theological fad regarding demon possession. During those years, demons became front-page stuff. Films like *The Exorcist, The Possession of Joel Delaney, The Omen* began to pour out of Hollywood. Not to be outdone by secular culture, Christians, both Evangelical and Catholic, went "demon-crazy." Scores of books were written, and religious radio and television programs were filled with the previously demon-possessed telling of their deliverance.

Amid this furor I found myself confronted by bizarre occurrences within my own congregation. In prayer groups, people often broke into fits of laughter, which they were powerless to control; sometimes their laughter would break up the prayer sessions. I remember retrieving one runaway teenager who had locked himself in a cheap hotel room and lost all clue to his identity. Indeed, he only returned to normal after another Christian joined me in praying for his deliverance. Then at last was he mentally adjusted enough to return to his parents.

But perhaps my greatest challenge came in January 1994 during evening worship. The service on that bitterly cold and snowy night was unusually well attended, in spite of a wind-chill index of around minus thirty. An odd young man, apparently in his early twenties, showed up at the service. He sat toward the back and made gentle flapping motions with his willowy arms. He was seated so far back that his antics were not noticed by most of the communicants. Of course, I did nothing to call attention to his behavior; I merely preached on one end of the congregation while he flapped on the other. But after the service I found him in the vestibule, too lightly dressed to go out into the bitter weather.

I asked him where he was from. He answered in an odd and far-away voice, more deeply basso than a normal voice should be. As he spoke, he continued to flap, and though his condition was lamentable, I had to stifle an awful urge to laugh. Realizing the gravity of the situation, I gained control of myself and found out his name and where he lived. Since he was determined to leave the building, I begged him not to go out into the night so inadequately clothed against the cold. At length, he left. I watched him through a frosted windowpane as he left the building. He went out and got into his car, which, though an old jalopy, started easily.

His otherworldly voice and his odd, psychotic behavior haunted me well into the night. I rose the next morning with the conviction that I should call his parents, if he had any, and tell them of his visit. I searched the telephone directory for the family name and called the number. When his father answered, I told him the story.

He thanked me and told me that his son had gotten up in the middle of the night and taken off all his clothes. In this naked condition, he had run through the house shrieking. His son was not a large man, but when the ambulance came, the orderlies could barely restrain him. After his arrival at the mental hospital, he was so violent he tore the heavy cyclone screens from the windows of his room. Only with strong drugs and a straight jacket was he at last subdued.

This was on the first day of January 1974. Throughout that year, several other events of this nature occurred in my life. In examining that critical year, I came to believe that neither psychology nor coincidence could explain these phenomena, and I developed a theology that I had not learned in all my years of theological training.

ᜃᜃᜃᜓ

C. S. Lewis once said that in respect to the devil we usually make one of two mistakes: we either give him undue attention or ignore him altogether. My intention is not to lead you to either of those extremes, but of this you may be sure: by inserting the letter *d* in front of the word *evil*, you will arrive at the word *devil*. Few people doubt the existence of evil, and many believe that its source is the devil.

Perhaps you recoil at that statement. Don't we all a bit? Such eerie propositions make us ask, "Is there really a devil? If so, who is he? Where did he come from?" As we seek answers, we will examine those sources within the Bible that discuss his origin (Ezekiel 28:15–18, Isaiah 14, Revelation 12, and others). But in seeking these answers we will avoid three extremes. First, we will ignore those current New-Age notions that good and evil originate from a common source. New-Age views of "one-source" for good and evil have been popularized in films such as *The Star Wars Trilogy*, in which Darth Vader and Obi-won—the good and evil icons of the films—have one common origin in "The Force," the single source of all living things. This idea is abhorrent to main-stream Christians.

Second, we will correct the tendency among contemporary mainstream theologians to "psychologize" demons, to see evil as real but demons as simply psychoses, neuroses, and the like. Evangelical preachers and theologians, by contrast, tend to take both demons and angels seriously and generally agree on both the origin and widespread existence of these spiritual creatures.

Third, we will avoid overestimating the demonic influence on the Christian life. For instance, one biblical idea that has been somewhat overblown is the idea that demons are territorial. As recently as the late eighties, a course on Signs and Wonders, complete with an academic catalogue number and curriculum, was offered at Pasadena's Fuller Theological Seminary. In this course, demons and exorcisms were a regular part of class study. In an article discussing this course, the *Los Angeles Times* had this to report:

> Under the militant banner of "spiritual warfare," growing numbers of evangelical and charismatic Christian leaders are preparing broad assaults on what they call the cosmic powers of darkness. Fascinated by the notion that Satan commands a hierarchy of territorial demons, some mission agencies and big-church pastors are devising strategies for breaking the "strongholds" of those evil spirits alleged to be controlling cities and countries.[1]

The concept of these territorial demons is often cat-alogued under the notion of territorial powers, or "prin-cipalities and strongholds," an idea that forms a basic part of the plot of Frank Peretti's immensely popular novels. C. Peter Wagner believes that Satan even assigns a demon or a host of demons to manage every geographical and political area of the globe.[2]

But the practice of pursuing these "ruling angels" often runs away with the temptation to see demons every-where. This preoccupation can foster a negative intrigue—with evil that is prone to eliminate the believ-er's positive focus on Christ. The idea that God appointed angels over all of the pagan nations is found in Daniel 10. The word *archon*, or ruling power, seems to indicate there are "principalities and powers," or demonic *archons*, as well. These powerful demons are the minions of Satan. They are malevolent beings in charge of the various nations, or for that matter neighborhoods of the world. One pastor in Illinois actually went into prayer and dis-putation with such territorial demons over the control of the various streets of neighborhoods within his parish.[3]

Some Excesses to Avoid

When tempted, no one should say, "God is tempting me." For God cannot be tempted by evil, nor does he tempt anyone.

JAMES 1:13

All of us are engaged in a never-ending battle with dark forces that harass our existence. No Christian has ever been exempt from these. But here are some roads you must not travel in your struggle with "the other kingdom." First, do not see all your trials and woes as demon-related. It may be less dramatic but probably more honest to call some of our difficulties mere *difficulties* and not devils. Correct your checkbook problems, for instance, without rebuking those "infesting checkbook demons." Deal with the issues of dysfunction without ordering the "demons of co-dependency" back into "the pit of hell." Christ wants you to know victorious living, dealing realistically with Satan, but you cannot do that if you "demonize" your problems while shrinking away from all-important spiritual disciplines. Demons—overemphasized—are not the way we deal with reality. They are often a way we escape it. In such escapism, we never live the deeper life—we abdicate it.

Paul knew countless honest struggles, but he did not need to call demons. Who has not known the struggle he describes in Romans 7? "For what I do is not the good I want to do; no, the evil I do not want to do—this I keep on doing. Now if I do what I do not want to do, it is no longer I who do it, but it is sin living in me that does it. . . . What a wretched man I am! Who will rescue me from this body of death?" (vv. 19–20, 24).

Second, remain in charge of your decision making. Christians too often believe that becoming a Christian puts Christ in the driver's seat of our lives, and from that moment on we are not responsible for our actions. Oh, that this were true! We must always remain soundly in charge of every decision of our lives. Certainly, when we become Christians, Christ becomes Lord, and his flawless counsel in our decision making is always available. He, the Hebrews 13:5 Christ, will always show us the right choices, but we alone must make the decisions.

Just as we tend to make Christ responsible for our good choices, we tend to blame Satan for our bad ones. Satan does not own our will; neither is he in charge of our lives. He exerts immense force in our lives, tempting us in order to destroy us, and of this you may be sure, just as Jesus has only the finest things in mind for us, so Satan will not be happy unless both our lives and the force of our Christian witness are destroyed. But just as Christ does not make good decisions for us, Satan does not make our bad ones. It is never honest to say, "The devil made me do it."

Third, don't make the devil a convenient scapegoat for your failures nor angels a platform for your successes. Your life is not that cosmic in its significance.

Still, in spite of these three warnings, we must not become so blasé that we cannot see that we live out the natural course of our lives between two very distinct powers. Our every obedience will please God. Our every disobedience will serve Satan. God wants us to have the most meaningful life possible and desires to place within you the joy of knowing you have chosen a life that is committed to Christ—a life filled with purpose. God longs to enable us to take upon ourselves the mantle of servant, and as servants we will begin to see as servants see. The world will become for us—as it was for Jesus—a needy place where the evil one has decimated all hope. And we will cherish every opportunity to restore that hope in the name of Jesus.

Seeing Things as They Are

Be strong in the Lord and in his mighty power.
Ephesians 6:10

If I learned anything during 1974, it was to let the Bible be my reply to Satan.

Once I was asked to lecture on communication at a small Christian college on the West Coast. As I flew west, the skies became increasingly cloudy, and when I arrived, a full-fledged storm was pounding the little campus with rain and hail. Later that night, after leaving the lecture hall, I returned to my room, which was in the most formidable guest house I had ever seen—a huge old house at the center of the campus. In the chilling rain I fumbled for my key as I approached the Victorian door. I managed to get the reluctant key in the lock and turned it. The door creaked open like a prop from *The Twilight Zone*. Reluctantly I stepped inside and closed the door. I wished I hadn't. Immediately, I felt a deep chill that went clear to the bone.

That night I understood that just as it is warm and wonderful to be filled with the Spirit of God, there is an equal and opposite feeling. This chill deepened from fear to terror as I climbed the creaky old stairs to my bedroom. The storm beat upon the house, and lightning created strobe explosions of weird shadows on peeling wallpaper. *Amityville* came to mind. Alone in the old house, I was an easy target for Satan, whose reality was self-proclaiming. Since I am not fond of patent exorcism phrases, I determined, as I entered my room, simply to quote Scripture into the oppressive darkness. I was surprised at how many Scriptures I could quote under such duress. Yet it worked well. When I had finished quoting about twenty minutes of the Bible, the terror eased. I fell into a refreshing and needful sleep. The storm raged on, but I slept. This experience, more than any other, taught me the great value in memorizing the Word of God.

From that night of confrontation, I can offer you a bit of counsel learned in the shadows to be practiced in the light: enjoy Christ. Bask in his love. Count his presence in your life the chief of all your joys. Let his reality lead you to a never-ending anthem of personal praise. But never forget that an opposite force is at work in your personal world. This personal devil can be stopped at the threshold of your security. Your commitment to and use of the Word of God is fearsome truth to the Father of Lies (John 8:44). His dark, intrusive force will always seek to invade your devotion. He will circle you with gloom to obscure those moral values that you learned from Christ in sunlight. Scripture will bring light to these fearsome shadows. Jesus will declare the path you should walk. The path of evil is rarely so clearly labeled.

Serving Christ brings with it such a clear sense of reward that it is never hard to see the immediate sense of wonder and fulfillment it provides. Not so with evil. It is clandestinely rooted in our own self-absorption. Because the devil is the Lord of "feel-good," he will teach us the fun of license rather than the power of self-denial. He comes with an easy morality-mark to show us how we can conveniently "re-label" those black areas of our morality as "gray." "Have you sinned?" he will ask. "Certainly not. You are feeling bad for no really healthy reasons," he will assure us. Soon his work will convince us what we were too eager to believe all along. We are not really sinners, are we? We merely "goof up" from time to time. How could we ever do anything "satanic?" We don't *really* sin. We only experience small negative infringements that are so common, they lay no real charge against grace. We are not transgressors, are we? Are not our little moral maneuvers so customary as to be typical on earth and trivial in heaven? Are not our sins boringly ordinary? When sins are so common, isn't is damaging to our self-esteem to be overly concerned about their consequence? Everybody does them. We do too. Why make a big deal about it? In the very ordinariness of our goof-ups, we're neither failing Jesus nor pleasing Satan, are we? There's nothing very cosmic about our boo-boos, is there? Shouldn't minimal sinning avoid the spiritual hypochondria of over-confessing? Like everyone else, we are merely getting by the best way possible, making our hard lives easier, our despair more meaningful, our dyspepsia less sour. By ignoring our own sin we are, in short, making life possible. I'm O.K. You're O.K. Sure, we still need Jesus but not to forgive us. We can do that on our own.

Mark this: we cannot achieve Christian maturity without dealing seriously with sin and its source. Only with such a realistic view can we learn to spot evil and the come-hither intrigue of the evil one. We will be victorious in the Christian life when we learn to see and determine to turn from those willful choices that destroy Christian living. Only when we have seen this can we measure the success or failure in our morality.

These seemingly innocent compromises rarely manifest themselves as evil. When we follow their spiraling lure into some horrible helix of despair we will begin to experience the demonic. Then we will feel the oppressive sense of evil, that we missed when we considered our compromises innocent or unimportant. Then we will have answers to such questions as: What made us act as we did? What made us behave so contrary to what we ever believed we could? Peter claimed that he would go to prison and to death before he would ever deny Christ (Luke 22:33). On the spot Christ warned him that human nature is fickle. It willingly serves Satan, in spite of its godly bravado (Luke 22:34). Jesus said Peter's godly intentions would fail even before the cock crowed.

Our disappointment in ourselves is as predictable as our strongest declarations. Which of us have not heard the cock crowing our failed, blustery promises? Do you not sin and tell Jesus you will "never, never, never" do that again? Then your resolve is brought by the enemy for a bargain bit of ego. Promise . . . failure . . . promise . . . failure—such is the disparaging routine. The condemning cock seldom crows without you being ready to make yet another promise and wait for another failure.

What is it that makes us claim to be true to Christ while we are in the process of acting so unchristlike? It is the will of the enemy. His will is so much more pleasurable, so void of real requirement that we long to do it. Only when we act so clearly against God's will do we come to know that our pretended innocence is more than mere moral naiveté. We were actually serving the will of the one who is set against our gracious Lord. We actually acted for Satan's pleasure instead of Christ's. Were we making these huge immoral decisions entirely on our own? Yes, but let's be honest: even as we did it, we were serving the Evil One. We were committed not only to our destruction but to that of every good thing in God's world.

The cliché is right: Satan *is* alive and well on planet earth. What is his will for your life? What would Satan like to see you become? Where will you be a year from now or ten years from now if he has his way? What about eternity? Is it there? If so, what are the ends he would like to stamp upon that incredible infinity of your life?

These are the larger questions that we must address. Satan is real, but beware lest you come to some unnatural (or supernatural) exaggeration of your importance in the world. Satan would love to sidetrack your positive walk with Christ into some negative erratic preoccupation with the occult. While I do not want to snare you into such paralyzing views of the spiritual realm, I do want to acquaint you with what Lewis Sperry Chafer called the "angelic conflict." Each of us must live our whole life between this ongoing "quarreling of angels": "For though we live in the world, we do not wage war as the world does. The weapons we fight with are not weapons of the world. On the contrary, they have divine power to demolish strongholds" (2 Corinthians 10:3–4). We do indeed live amid these immense forces of good and evil, always wrestling against principalities and powers (Ephesians 6:12).

In this ongoing spiritual warfare, you are responsible for both your own decisions and the outcome of your life. Every good decision of your life must be made in Christ's name, for it has given pleasure to God. In the Bible, God is called the giver of "every good and perfect gift" (James 1:17), while Satan is called the "father of lies" (John 8:44). We are to serve God, and repudiate the devil.

But how do you make this happen? Work hard at the issue of biblical authority. Do not feed your soul on any spurious phobias you have about Satan. Don't develop within you any nonbiblical, nightmarish fears or dark manias. Do you have supernatural fears? At some time in life all of us do. Meet those fears with the force of Holy Scripture. Let the biblical truth order those terrors back into the abyss where they were hatched. Avoid books that trivialize Satan by making him a mere ghost story filled with titillating horrors of "things that go bump in the night." There are plenty of such volumes in print, taking up too much shelf space in less-discriminating libraries. The world does not need another glitzy *National*

Enquirer tabloid look at "The Exorcism of Elvis" or "Demon Speaks Out of New Born Baby" or "Unsuspecting Apollo Astronauts Bring Back Hitchhiking Lunar Poltergeist."

Ultimately, I know of only two steps to being victorious over Satan. First, we must be both indwelt and, second, overlaid. That is, we must be indwelt by fullness of Christ in the person of his Holy Spirit. Then we must be protected by mentally overlaying our frail will-power with the armor of God.

We must have the Spirit of God (Ephesians 3:17) living inside us. The Apostle Paul gave us the recipe for welcoming this inner Christ:

> Your attitude should be the same as that of Christ Jesus: Who, being in very nature God, did not consider equality with God something to be grasped, but made himself nothing, taking the very nature of a servant, being made in human likeness. And being found in appearance as a man, he humbled himself and became obedient to death—even death on a cross! Therefore God exalted him to the highest place and gave him the name that is above every name, that at the very name of Jesus every knee should bow, in heaven and on earth and under the earth, and every tongue confess that Jesus Christ is Lord, to the glory of God the Father. (Philippians 2:5–11)

Once we have welcomed the inner Christ, the second step of victory lies in clothing ourselves with strength. This formidable clothing is what Paul called "armor": "Put on the full armor of God so that you can take your stand against the devil's schemes" (Ephesians 6:11).

I had a friend who for years used to get up every morning and mentally imagine himself dressing in the uniform of the day. He first put on the belt of truth (Ephesians 6:14) and asked God to help him live in utter integrity. Next, as the Scripture suggests he would put on the breastplate of righteousness (Ephesians 6:14); as he did so he would ask that God would take from him all self-righteousness and fill him with that righteousness which is by faith, just as Abraham once "believed God, and it was credited to him as righteousness" (Galatians 3:6). Next he would imagine himself putting on the combat boots of peace (Ephesians 6:15). All day long he would quote to himself the beatitude: "Blessed are the peacemakers, for they will be called sons of God" (Matthew 5:9). Then he imagined himself taking up the shield of faith, as he committed himself to the entire Gospel; his commitment was to nothing less than the whole gospel. He strengthened his life to "contend for the faith that was once for all entrusted to the saints" (Jude 1:3). Then, as surely as though he was standing before a dressing mirror, he placed upon his head the helmet of salvation. He thanked God that he had been chosen to proclaim "the praises of him who called you out of darkness into his wonderful light" (1 Peter 2:9). Finally he took up the sword of the Spirit, which is the Word of God (Ephesians 6:17).

He said that as he dressed he realized that of the six pieces of armor mentioned in Ephesians 6, five of them were there to protect the believer from the fiery darts of the wicked one (Ephesians 6:16). Only the final one—the sword of the Spirit—was given as a weapon of advance. After he was fully dressed and protected by spiritual armor, he picked up the sword of the Word of God. He was then ready to move out into a godless culture, changing his world with the claims of Christ.

The Sword of Our Advance

Take the helmet of salvation and the sword of the Spirit, which is the word of God.

EPHESIANS 6:17

The word "sword" in this passage comes from the Greek word *machaira*. The *machaira* was a special sword carried by the Roman infantry, with a firm hilt and a short blade sharpened on both sides. Though short, the *machaira* was used by Rome to conquer the entire world. Often when foreign armies—who carried longer swords—saw the Roman infantry advancing with these short swords, they were tempted to laugh. But the Romans were confident fighters. They knew short swords worked better in close combat, where the longer swords were unwieldy and ineffective. The *machaira* cut well in close combat.

Make no mistake. "The word of God is living and active. Sharper than any double-edged sword [*machaira*], it penetrates even to dividing soul and spirit, joints and marrow; it judges the thoughts and attitudes of the heart" (Hebrews 4:12). Satan trembles when he sees Christians who are skilled in their knowledge and use of the Word of God, as he does when he sees even the weakest of saints upon their knees. While prayer causes tremors in the foundation of hell, Bible-study is the sword of our offense against those ancient battlements that rise upon those foundations.

Here then is your strategy for victory. *Indwelt* by Christ and *overlaid* by the armor, you are called to do battle with the entire realm of evil. Pray unceasingly. Make the *machaira* of the Word your continual preoccupation. Then you need never fear him who was cast down to earth in fury. Neither do you inordinately need to fear those creatures of fury who serve him. Your confident living knows no real threat. The Cross has taken care of them all. And where the wood rose and the blood fell, the earth opened to swallow up all your fears and intimidation. You are free. The responsibility for moral living is still yours, but the responsibility for winning the big war is his. Be confident of your victory, for as the poet wrote:

> *Hell's foundations quiver, at the shout of praise,*
> *Brothers lift your voices, loud your anthems raise.*

Years ago Paul Billheimer helped us conclude that we are *Destined for the Throne*. How altogether wonderful is this truth. But eternity is not our only arena of victory. We are also destined to win in the here and now, by being filled with the Spirit and being overlaid with armor of God.

With this simple recipe of victory, let us turn to the issue of your own spiritual pilgrimage. Christ is within you, the armor of your warfare is around you. You have won. You are winning. You will win. Your victory is so certain that defeat is unthinkable.

2

THE FURY OF ANGELS

Therefore rejoice, you heavens and you who dwell
in them! But woe to the earth and the sea, because
devil has gone down to you! He is filled with fury,
because he knows that his time is short.

REVELATION 12:12

A friend of mine came home from Vietnam psychologically destroyed. Though he had received only minor wounds, he was so emotionally scarred that it was hard to believe he was not more physically wounded. His inward wounds were so deep that he would sometimes break into tears over the terror his young eyes had seen. He was often quiet and withdrawn. His life was riddled with things too frightening to talk about. Any sudden noise would jar him into dark reveries that left him incommunicado for hours. He carried the war around inside him, and his private Vietnam was so costly that he was only able to win it one day at a time.

Many believers fight such wars. The horror is real, dark, inward, fearsome; its casualties are many. Its battlefields are sudden and furious, and its wounds are divorce-court deep and visceral. The wounded cry and wait for healing while they hide in fear from the next encounter. They appear to be in charge but know they are not. They spend their lives trying to find anyone who will help them define their conflict and name their enemy.

These small, private battles come from a larger conflict that few of the wounded ever suspect. This ancient war between God and Satan, however, is not between love and hate but between love and anger. Hate is Satan's attitude toward God—but it can never be God's attitude toward Satan or any other being. God is love—totally love—(1 John 4:8), and as such he is incapable of hate. Satan was cast out of heaven because he exalted himself against God. He had to go not because God hated him but because God would not force him to continue in a relationship of love that he no longer desired. Even the anger of God, often called "the wrath of god," is not a tantrum, some cheap emotional loss of divine control. Nor is the anger of God a grudge. God's anger is, as the theologians say, righteous indignation, a holy reaction to unholy wrong.

What lay behind Satan's expulsion from heaven? The holiness of God. God and heaven are both holy with a kind of purity that admits no hint of stain. God's anger derives from the hurt he feels in knowing that those he loves have rebelled against him. This broken heart of God yearns to restore those in rebellion. Satan's leaving heaven does not leave God perpetually glowering down upon Satan—such enduring anger would be merely a grudge, and a grudge can find no place in the holiness of God.

But mark this, a grudging human heart can be the root system that blossoms in satanic fruit. It can be a secret wound that keeps a person from true spiritual wholeness. For the past eleven years a pastor friend of mine has preached to a man I will call Hiram Smith, a man in his early seventies. Hiram never misses church but sits through every service with his fingers stuck in his ears. He never takes them out throughout the service. Why?

Eleven years ago Hiram opposed—in a heated business meeting—a motion to install a new sound system in the church. Hiram lost—and for eleven years now has sat week after week, making sure his opposition is never forgotten. What Hiram can't see is that he has come under the control of a demonic force that always comes to church with him.

Some years ago, Luella, differing from the rest of the music committee, voted to buy a Rogers Organ. The rest of them wanted an Allen Organ. Luella believed that I, as her pastor, supported the "godless" action of the committee, and she became angry with me. Her anger caused her to regard me in a most distant manner. She wouldn't speak to me in the church. She waged a ruthless blitz of gossip among her friends, who by odd coincidence also believed that God had led us to buy a Rogers Organ.

For four years Luella said nothing good about me to anyone. She turned from every opportunity to bid me a good day in the halls of the church or in the streets of our town. During an evangelistic rally, a visiting evangelist ended his sermon by calling on each of us to go to anyone who might have something against us and ask them to pray with us for reconciliation. In fact, the evangelist asked us to seek their forgiveness even if the offense was theirs. So I mustered all the courage I could and went to Luella. I asked her if she could forgive me and join me in prayer.

"Pastor, I could never pray with you. Remember, I wanted a Rogers Organ and you chose to stand against me. In fact, I feel uncomfortable that you've come to me in this service to call attention to me by letting others see me refuse you in this service."

"Well, Luella," I replied, "I want to pray with you, whether or not you will pray with me." Without waiting for her to ask me not to, I began quietly, "Lord, I thank you for my sister, Luella. She has been faithful to your church and has blessed so many of us with her great musical talent. Bless her life and her family. May she enjoy your love in the fullest possible way. In Jesus name, amen." When I rose from the pew, Luella still had that firm, hard look that as far as I know still characterizes her wintry expression in church.

Why does she come to church? I suspect that she derives some kind of pleasure from exhibiting displeasure. Does she suspect that she has given Satan a little foothold in her life? I am confident that she believes she is a good Christian and would never knowingly serve the devil. Yet grudge is the constant and willful tolerance of a demonic prejudice. It can be so constant and become so customary that those who allow it finally see it as a normal way of life. They unwittingly make it such a part of their lives, that to live without it would cause them to experience an odd emptiness.

God's love is constant. He created Satan in love, and he maintains a holy, grieving disappointment at seeing this lost archangel make choices that first caused his fall from heaven. God is more a disappointed parent than a grudging judge. Hell is a place for Satan: the fiery torment of the place is not flames that God put there because he enjoys seeing Satan and all who follow him tortured forever. Rather, Satan chose hell as his own dwelling place outside the circle of divine love. Hell is the only place where God isn't, nor can he ever be. Anywhere God isn't, will be a place of torment. It can't be anything else. Separation from God puts the torment in the flame and the suffering in the sulfur.

But what of demons?

Demons are but angels who fell with their exiled lord. They were washed out of heaven in the wake of Lucifer's Pride. A third of all angels knew instant exile with Satan. John Milton spends a great deal of time discussing these wailing demons. In *Paradise Lost* this odd gathering of losers sit on the heights, bewailing all that they have lost. They are a horrid host of exiles to whom heaven is forever banned. The very mention of all that they have lost is the eternal lament of these embittered spirits.

But what these fallen angels felt is a common feeling to all who love God and want to please him. How are we to get past our own painful feelings that we have let God down because of our sins? Remember that only two courses are open to us in ridding ourselves of the feeling that we have disappointed God. First, we may find a kind of spiritual remorse that festers in self-focus. This was Judas' Iscariot's problem. He committed suicide because he could not undo his betrayal and sought no forgiveness from Christ (Matthew 27:3–10). Peter, on the other hand, confesses Christ once for every act of betrayal (John 21:15–19) and is restored. Our remorse over our failure to honor Christ will always end in one of these two ways: the pleasure of renewed fellowship with Christ (like Peter) or the utter desolation of broken, unforgiven promises (like Judas). Everyone here and there serves Satan. Remorse over our spiritual failures never need be terminal.

Anger: The Essential Character of Satan

Then the dragon was enraged ...

REVELATION 12:17

I love Spain, but I do not attend bullfights. I hate to see the torturing of the animals. This pageant, enjoyed

37

by so many, seems to speak of a horrible and universal enjoyment of watching other living things suffer. First the *toreros* cut the shoulder muscles of the bull to weaken him, then the *picadors* spear him with the brightly colored *banderillas*. The maddened animal becomes furious. In this fury he is released to deal with the *torero*. The Bible teaches us that Satan and his hosts (Revelation 12:12) were long ago "released in fury." This fearsome, super-natural rage is the picture of all that the Christian faces in dealing with Satan. Such hostile anger forges the arena of our spiritual warfare.

Nearly all who study demon possession say that those who are possessed exhibit feats of superhuman strength. Consider the young man I mentioned earlier, who tore the screens off the windows of his hospital room. In Peter Blatty's novel *The Exorcist*, the demoniac—a young ado-lescent girl—throws a priest out of the window of her room. I once talked to a thin adolescent boy who was able, when under the control of his demonic force, to throw huge pieces of furniture about the room. It is as though they are not filled merely with beings of hate but beings of fury. The devil's rage is not an orderly focused anger like the wrath of God might be. It is, under the rag-ing influence of these creatures of fury, more like instant tantrums that grow from grudge and erupt in uncon-trollable outbursts of rage. Remember the Gerasene demoniac in Luke 8? The Bible says that in his anger he broke chains and no man could control his rage.

But consider not just the relationship between grudge and tantrum but the relationship between pride and anger. This relationship is rooted in every Biblical pas-sage that discusses the origin of evil. Pride was that foun-tain that began in the plazas of heaven and ended in the abyss. The essential character of Satan was arrogance. He was fiercely proud and thought to exalt his throne above the stars (Isaiah 14:12–15). His pride, as is usually the case, gave way to anger. Once cast out of heaven he came down to the earth furious in his descent (Revelation 12:12). His anger was multiplied by those angels who fell with him, for in being cast out of heaven "his tail swept a third of the stars" (Revelation 12:4), or one third of heaven's host. These embittered beings became his minions bent on the same fury.

Job 1 is an evidence that Satan can instantly unleash his pent-up fury against anyone at any time. In a single chapter he destroys Job's family and all his vast financial empire. All that Job counted dear in life is demolished at the caprice of satanic fury. Such evil fury is depicted in the various names of Satan. He is called or implied to be:

Abaddon, the destroyer, Revelation 9:11
the accuser, Revelation 12:10
the adversary, 1 Peter 5:8
the murderer, John 8:44
the evil one, Matthew 13:19
the trickster, Ephesians 6:11
the trapper, 2 Timothy 2:26

All of these various names imply that earth's angry enemy is bent against every act of good will. To the church of Pergamos John wrote, "I know where you live—where Satan has his throne" (Revelation 2:13). The implication is that Pergamos was the very center of Satan's fury that was devouring the church.

Just who is Satan? He is not some vague idea of malevolence—no mere philosophical personification of evil. Rather, he is the thrashing and wounded serpent of

Scripture. His anger leaves him completely unmanageable in the merely human milieu. You do not have to turn to novelized satanic tales to recognize just how furious he is. These fictional Satans can merely furnish you with titillating and intriguing images. These Frankenstein images may make us afraid of the dark, but they lack the theological force to make us consider the real horror of evil—eternal loss and complete separation from God. It isn't that Satan makes us fear the dark, he can literally damn us eternally to darkness. He can and does use political institutions to help him bar the gates to salvation. Therefore, I would have you consider the real and horrible historical force of the angry dragon.

Satan's Fury: In Political Institutions

The beast was given a mouth to utter proud words.... And he was given authority over every tribe, people, language and nation.

REVELATION 13:5, 7

The killing fields of the Khmer Rouge, the savage tribal massacres of Rwanda-Burundi, the Indonesian anti-Communist purge, the horror of Stalin's collectivizations: these events indicate more about the power of Satan's fury than scary devil movies. The most immense fury of Satan can only be registered in these grand historical ways.

If you would identify the Father of Fear see the terror of his evil anger in the pathos of children made afraid: the fear of African-American children crossing white picket-lines in Selma, Alabama, or the Jewish child who comes to understand the horror of the Nazi swastika. Recognize anti-Semitic horrors of Minsk, when a poor woman standing deep in a trench, on the dead bodies of her friends, holds up her child to Adolph Eichmann and says, "Shoot me, but please take my baby!" Eichmann reaches as though to take her child. Then suddenly he draws his hands back in brusque refusal and orders the rifle fire. The first retort of the rifle cuts the baby into blood, and the second folds mother and child together into the same trench. The drone of a bulldozer buries every semblance of Third Reich humanity. Such signs are the global evidence of Satan's evil fury.

So as we consider the nature of demons, let us see them in terms of their horrible power as expressed through human institutions. How do these demons oppress vast continents of people? Franz Hinkelamert says that governments and institutions do this by what he calls the "thingification" of persons. Both governments and institutions "thingify" when they reduce people to mere things that destroy their humanity and replace it with economics or power abuse.[1]

Along with the rest of the world, I was incensed in 1980 by the cruel assassination of Bishop Romero in El Salvador. It was easy to love Romero. His Christlike demeanor enabled him to walk compassionately through the poor of his country, siding with them instead of the small and wealthy ruling class. Romero's El Salvador was so poor that America's McDonalds franchise had a larger annual income than his entire nation. Estimates of those who disappeared in the night and those who were more blatantly killed by governmental death squads run as high as seventy thousand.

The city garbage dump became the killing fields of Latin America. Liberationist priests often took up guns to help the poor defend themselves against the powerful. Romero refused to carry arms to stand against the village massacres and remote assassinations. In the wake of these tremors of terror, Romero became the Ghandi of El Salvador. He walked through defiant militia, armed with all kinds of military hardware, and offered Mass for the peasants. Just the sight of this man the hope of an entire village would quicken. He was assassinated—like Thomas Becket of old—as he stood on the altar serving communion to his people.

Why? Because he refused to let his government turn people into things. It is easy to murder people once you subtract their humanity. Slaughterhouses are cheerfully served by employees who kill only things. But people are not things to be used for whatever purposes tyrants might connive. It is a demonic strategy to make one's enemies less than human and then destroy them because they have no humanity. It is easy to kill what we have thingified.

Jesus must have won the hearts of his own country because he saw the true worth of every person. Because he realized that prejudice precedes every act of dehumanization, he told prejudice-smashing stories: one of a very *good* Samaritan (Luke 10) and another of a very grateful Samaritan leper (Luke 17:16). Jesus even conducted a preaching tour in this despised land (John 4). This would be no less significant than a southern evangelist opening a crusade in Selma, Alabama, in 1950.

In the early decades of this century white Christians often justified their racism by citing Genesis 9:25, saying that African-Americans bore the "curse of Ham." Now that Christian scholarship has matured, we would never think of saying that. But what about some evangelicals' prejudices toward women? Many still cite Ephesians 5:22 and 1 Peter 3:1 as evidence that women should "remain silent in the churches" (1 Corinthians 14:34) and let the men run things. This idea coupled with super-macho egoism has led men to put down women, telling sexist jokes about dumb blondes or women drivers. I believe that someday all evangelicals will repudiate the use of the Bible to justify gender prejudice just as they have come to repudiate the use of the Bible to justify racial prejudice. May God hasten the day, when we quit "thingifying" people so we can abuse anyone for any reason.

Gender prejudice is not new. An old Jewish proverb in the time of Christ was often repeated by men to justify both gender and racial prejudice: "I thank God that I am neither a woman, a dog, nor a Gentile." My favorite prejudice-smashing event from the life of Jesus is often overlooked (or consciously bypassed) by many preachers. On one occasion Jesus was in the land of Tyre and Sidon. A Gentile woman—whom most Jews considered to be dogs—came to him, begging him to have pity on her demon-possessed daughter. Jesus tried to explain that, while he loved all people, he had come as a Jew to work his miracles among the Jews. Jesus answered not as he felt but in terms of the popular Jewish prejudices of the day. "It is not right to take the children's bread and toss it to their dogs!" But the woman took the popular prejudice and turned it back toward Jesus, "Yes, Lord, . . . but even the dogs eat the crumbs that fall from their masters' table" (Matthew 15:21–28). Jesus was touched and healed the woman's daughter.

Oh, the misery that is caused by dehumanizing people! Prejudice rises from hell as sure as love descends from heaven. This may be why Jesus reacts so severely to James and John when they want to call down fire from heaven on an inhospitable Samaritan village. Jesus tells them plainly that he had not come to reinforce human hatred but to save all who would be saved (Luke 9:56). Jesus directly assigns the ungodly desires of James and John as demonic: "You do not know what kind of spirit you are of" (Luke 9:55—later textual inclusion), he told them. Only when they quit seeing Samaritans as people could they really desire to destroy them—that desire was clearly not of the Spirit of God, said Jesus. Thingification is always the work of demons.

Walter Wink tells of a four-month trip he took to several South America countries in the early eighties. He did not stay in posh American hotels but in *barrios* and *favelas* where he watched people deal with the everyday crush of civil oppression. Such people often simply disappeared quietly in the night. Wink talked to people who had been tortured. He was so affected by the evil of civil systems that he confessed that he at last became ill. He testified: "The evils we encountered were so monolithic, so massively supported by our own government, and in some cases so anchored in a long history of tyranny, that it scarcely seemed that anything could make a difference."[2]

Such political oppression displays the real nature of spiritual warfare against the Almighty. Many German theologians at the outset of World War II believed that the inherent evil of the Third Reich brought with it into Germany a personification of evil that one could feel and see in the streets. Karl Heim and Otto Piper believed that there was an inrush of all sorts of demonic activities around the rise of Adolph Hitler. Both Emil Brunner and C. S. Lewis, who wrote his famous *Screwtape Letters* during this historical era, believed that the genocidal horrors of those years awakened all to the reality of the demonic realm. Dale Moody, the late Baptist Theologian, said that the horrors of the Third Reich can only be explained in terms of a personal devil. Otherwise it is not possible to harmonize such horrors with the ordinary pious and amiable people one comes to know in modern Germany. The same might be said of race riots. Among the working class or even the elite, the normative and genial behavior of Americans is difficult to harmonize with the savage and murderous fury of some civil protests and rioters.[3]

The common horrors of humanity's inhumanity, it seems to me, often eclipse these international horrors with deeds so savage they can be accounted for in no other way but in terms of the villainy of Satan. As Dr. Tom Dooley said,

> There's no other explanation for some of the things the Communists did. Like the priest who had eight nails driven into his skull. . . . And there were the seven little boys and their teacher. They were praying the *Our Father* when soldiers came upon them. One soldier whipped out his bayonet and sliced off the teacher's tongue. The other took chopsticks and drove them into the ears of the seven little boys. How do you treat cases like that?[4]

Such inhumanity is rooted in demonic soil. Cruelty that enjoys the suffering it spawns is born of hell. There is no other explanation.

The Nature of Love and Anger

With this in mind, be alert and always keep on praying . . .

EPHESIANS 6:18

The human outrage that marks such civic villainy can be seen, of course, in simpler ways. What of those vile and

45

evil serial killers whose lust for blood can have no source at all in good? Satan must be the source of the horrors that live in America's streets. The drug war, the drive-by killings, where nothing can explain the random terror but the existence of Satan. For those who would rather cite the more exotic evidences of evil the examples are endless. The hostility of the Charles Manson murders, the fourteen witches hanged at Salem, the fury of the Spanish inquisition with its horrible tortures. The modern children murdered in silent abductions at black masses; the flaming finish of the Branch Davidians in Waco, Texas; the Oklahoma City bombing—do not each of these tell us of the reality of an evil that exists beyond mere casual or psychological rationalizations?

Milton was right. Satan and his minions are in reality furious beings, marked by power and a desire to get even with God. What characterizes Satan is both anger and hate. Anger is that unbridled emotional storm that makes one unpredictable and dangerous. Hate is that furious contempt that feeds on vengeance. Hate in league with temper makes Satan's fury hard to handle.

God, as we've already said, is incapable of hate. The Apostle's counsel is true, "God is love" (1 John 4:8). Hosea 11 defines the love of God. No good human parent ever hates his children. Neither does God, the divine parent, hate his children. Children may make their parents angry, but good parents can never be angered to the point that they would enjoy seeing their children suffer. Certainly good parents could never become so angry they would enjoy destroying their children. God, likewise, is not a parent who would stand at the brink of hell and enjoy the anguish of those who have chosen to reject him. Parents grieve their children's disobedience and disaffection. Our temporary flights of permissiveness into the will of Satan do not make God hate us. They do not even make God angry with us to the extent he would enjoy seeing us punished in hell. They rather grieve God, and grief is a love word. For this reason Paul counseled us, "And do not grieve the Holy Spirit of God, with whom you were sealed for the day of redemption" (Ephesians 4:30). We who have received Christ may not rile God in anger against us, but we may hurt God. Is he not our Divine Parent? Is he not the Father of our Lord Jesus? Has he not loved us with an everlasting love? Yes, yes. But it is his love for us that so much leaves God vulnerable to pain. He loves us so much that it is easy to break his heart. It is not possible to raise his anger to the point that he would lock us from heaven or seal us forever in the abyss. Hell was not primarily created for people, but for Satan. Those who never know Christ will spend eternity in hell, but God will find no joy in this destiny of their own choosing.

There are two Greek words for anger. One is the word *thumos* (found in Romans 2:8), which describes the erratic and temper-ridden ebb and flow of human anger. The other is *orgé*, which is used to designate God's fixed and settled anger toward evil. This kind of anger does not involve God in a furious loss of self-control. Neither, as I said earlier, is it a grudge. God never gets mad and in his rage damns either Satan or sinners. His settled disposition of judgment is as constant as his nature. We are not to assume that God has uncontrollable rages of wrath in which he looses his self-control and knocks the disobedient around in uncontrollable tantrums. But he will consistently judge both sin and Lucifer, the lord of sin, with *orgé*.

The wrath of God is fixed forever toward Satan. Christians are never to presume against God's supposed indulgence. God is not a grandparent that forever winks at sin. Paul asks forthrightly,

> So when you, a mere man, pass judgment on them and yet do the same things, do you think you will escape God's judgment? Or do you show contempt for the riches of his kindness, tolerance and patience, not realizing that God's kindness leads you toward repentance?
>
> But because of your stubbornness and your unrepentant heart, you are storing up wrath against yourself for the day of God's wrath.... (Romans 2:3–5)

How then are we to regard the bad things we do? What is their cost to our security in Christ after we are saved?

There is a level of human evil that so presumes against God that it sins against his holy love. "What shall we say, then? Shall we go on sinning so that grace may increase? By no means! We died to sin; how can we live in it any longer?" (Romans 6:1–2). Those who receive salvation need to receive it as eternal. But we must not brag so much about being saved that we begin to demonstrate a loose lifestyle that sees our sins of no consequence. How shameful would be the child who so depends upon his parent's love that he is cruel or physically brutal to them, knowing they love him so much they would never do anything to stand against his cruelties. Such a child is hardly worthy of the name "child" and has become a demonic monster. Are not all those who live in sin, never feeling sorry for the way they are hurting God, also monsters of a sort? Is not their great transgression their congenial self-excusing? They are parasites that eat the heart of grace. Their apathy is essentially evil.

Paul must have seen this horrible imbalance in two of his companions, named Hymenaeus and Alexander. These two one-time friends of his had made shipwreck of their good consciences toward God. Speaking of those who made grace shipwreck, he wrote, ". . . Hymenaeus and Alexander, whom I have handed over to Satan to be taught not to blaspheme" (1 Timothy 1:20). Those who serve Satan with no remorse about all that they have done to God's grace may at last be left to the horror of having to deal with Satan beyond any protestation of God's grace.

We must never excuse our sinfulness and thus become pawns of the devil. For the moment we begin to consider any of our sins as of no consequence, we are already under the control of the devil. This must not be so. The devil need never control us. He can always be beaten in the name of the Savior. Therefore, as we go out to do battle against Satan, let us remember that the only way to win in spiritual warfare is to wrap ourselves in grace.

And how do we wrap ourselves in God's protective love? Prayer is the wrapping of our protection. However we define spiritual warfare, we would be wise to define our Christian armor in terms of prayer. Frank Peretti's novels, while in some sense trivializing demons as macho boogie-men, emphasizes that prayer is the last line of real defense against these horrible creatures.

Paul Billheimer reminds us that to those destined for the throne "prayer is where the action is. Any church without a well organized and systematic prayer program is simply operating a religious treadmill."[5]

God and Satan Are Not Equals

When Jesus had called the Twelve together, he gave the power and authority to drive out all demons.

LUKE 9:1

Most irrational fears of Satan are borne out of the mistaken idea that God and Satan are equal and opposite powers. Those abnormally afraid of the devil see God as the white power and Satan as an equal and opposite black power. This black-white dualism fosters a cold and paralyzing terror of the evil one. Such dualists view God as being on an equal plane with Satan. No view could be more false.

Indeed, the devil has immense power—but only in respect to humans. In respect to God—and all of those who are filled with Christ—Satan's power is evil but minimal. From God's perspective, Satan has already been judged and thrown out of heaven (Revelation 12:12; Isaiah 14:12 and following), so the New Testament assumes that God has completely stripped the adversary of all power. Not only is God in charge of this inferior demiurge, but so is the man or woman who is filled with the Savior. In James 4:7, the brother of our Lord counsels us, "Resist the devil, and he will flee from you." This is offered as a promise to everyone who is filled with Christ. There is in this passage no hint of fear that we shall be defeated by the devil over whom we have been given the absolute power of resistance.

Only those outside of Christ need to consider Satan a formidable foe. It seems odd that many atheists, while doubting God, seem most reluctant to doubt Satan. The issue of atheism is only brought up once in the entire

Bible, where the very idiocy of th[...]
poet: "The fool says in his hea[...]
(Psalm 14:1). So why do those wh[...]
deny God not also deny Satan? P[...]
irrational fear that he might yet gai[...]
ing soul. It must appear to them t[...]
tle is safer than doubting too muc[...]

Christopher Marlowe's story o[...] is fiction,
but it is a kind of universal truth—myth. The impudence
of the scholar making deals with the devil in exchange
for his soul is a common theme in the literature of many
nations. But Faustus under the control of Mephistophe-
les comes to that fearsome end that accompanies all who
give up God to serve Satan. Even as they are dragged off
to hell, the deplorable state of their lostness is a plagu-
ing realization that gives birth to agonizing fear.

In 1974, the film *The Exorcist* gave birth to an irrational national phobia about demon possession. In the
wake of the film there was a bizarre rash of demonic inva-
sions reported. Demons may not have possessed as many
people as it seemed like in those days, but they did possess
the talk shows and tabloids for the better part of a decade.
Most psychiatrists pooh-poohed the notion of demon-
possession by saying that those who didn't pay their exorcist might be "repossessed." Even psychiatrists, however,
were at a loss to explain the psychoses of many of their
patients without at least considering the supernatural.

In the Blatty's original novel, and the film based on
it, Pazuzu, an ancient Assyrian demiurge, is a demon
released from an amulet in a near-eastern archaeological
dig. This demon came to Regan MacNeil through the
planchette—the movable pointer—of her Ouija board.
As the planchette moved, Pazuzu took control, calling

tain Howdy. From this gentle beginning the
then possessed the teenage girl and later, it
d, the whole nation. So popular was the film that
ike many theater-goers, was only able to secure tick-
ets for a post-midnight showing.

Such wee-morning movie showings spawned even
more irrational fears. Contagion reigned. Many came to
believe themselves demon-possessed and thronged the
offices of priests and pastors and psychiatrists. I was the
pastor of a large midwestern church in those days. One
of the young mothers in my church went to see this movie.
I was called by this parish mother in the middle of the
night. This ordinary, loving mother was hysterically shouting and crying into the receiver of the phone that her
three-year-old daughter was demon possessed. She said
her baby had been shouting obscenities at her in a deep
basso demonic voice (just like in the movie). She was so
certain of this that I quickly drove to their suburban home.

When I arrived, I found a petrified three-year-old girl
cowering in one corner of the room with her mother
shouting terrible anti-demonic exorcism phrases from the
other corner. The very small frightened child was so par-
alyzed by her mother's loud and confusing hysteria that
it is hard for me not to believe such an event would mark
the terrified child for life. I was finally able to coax the
frightened child into my arms and took her from that horrible room. I had the oddest feeling that the whole bizarre
event was indeed demonic. But the demonic element was
more in the psychotic behavior of the mother and the hellish fear with which she had traumatized her own child.

I could understand the effect that the movie had on
this hapless mother, however. I remembered my own feelings while sitting in that past-midnight theater, viewing

52

that film. Every time the priest approached the door of the demon-possessed Regan, I found myself inwardly bracing for a new round of horror. Finally the intermittent horror of the film merged into one long assault on my terrorized psyche. I remember the grateful feeling I had when at last, mercifully, the film was over. I will never forget how good it felt to leave the theater and go back out on the street and begin looking for my car. I still remember feeling light and airy. I had known that wonderful sensation only a few times before. I had felt that way when I first was born again, when I walked out of that small tent revival where I knew the exhilaration of salvation. Yet this time I was only walking out of a dark "demonic" theater. I remember feeling wonderfully odd in seeing the neon sign over a huge store that read simply "SEARS"! How great it felt just knowing that Sears and other "wonderfully normal" things were still a part of a "wonderfully normal" world. My exhilaration was almost jubilant when I realized that like most other department stores, the Sears store probably had a store-wide sales promo going; probably tube socks and things like that were on sale. I was delirious with all such simple possibilities.

After seeing *The Exorcist*, I found myself edgy about the whole idea of the demonic. Sears store or not, I didn't sleep well after leaving the movie.

But two wonderful Scriptures came to me. First, I remembered 1 John 4:4 (NKJV), "Greater is He that is in you, than he that is in the world." Here was one gloriously short verse containing two "he's": the first was a capital *He* and the second a lowercase *he*. I knew quite simply that the answer to our fears of the little *he* was to be sure that we are filled with the capital *He*.

The other Scripture was 1 John 4:1–3:

> Dear friends, do not believe every spirit, but test the spirits to see whether they are from God, because many false prophets have gone out into the world. This is how you can recognize the Spirit of God: Every spirit that acknowledges that Jesus Christ has come in the flesh is from God, but every spirit that does not acknowledge Jesus is not from God. This is the spirit of the antichrist which you have heard is coming and even now is already in the world.

What was so splendid about this particular Scripture is that it is so matter of fact. There is no admonition to fear evil spirits, just to identify them. The implication is that once we have identified them, we may go on about our business for they are no threat to us. If you proceed to 1 John 4:4, you have the full promise that there is no contest, for greater is the power of the indwelling Christ than the oft-noisy but powerless spirit of the adversary.

Avoiding the Lure of the Exotic

Then the man who had the evil spirit jumped on them and overpowered them all. He gave them such a beating that they ran out of the house naked and bleeding.

ACTS 19:16

The lure of the exotic is a wonderful spur to our imagination. In this day of corporate clout, many people like to imagine themselves as more powerful than they are. This lust for supernatural power seems to be overprevalent among Christians these days as well. It is somehow flattering to think ourselves able to utter certain rituals of exorcism and command vast legions of demons. This exotic power seems to fascinate some Christians. One writer suggests a fourfold, tidy sequence of steps by which any Christian can order demons around.[6] Graham Powel suggests there are thirteen Scriptures on the blood of Christ that demons hate to hear.[7] Citing Scriptures on the blood is not necessarily a weak formula for putting demons in their place, but it smacks of magic and formula that has not looked solely to the power of Christ to do what somehow we think we are able to do with a single "Shazam!" picked up in a $2.98 paperback from a bargain table in the Christian book store.

But any scheme that sets out various plans to make us master of Satan needs to be eyed with suspicion. Trying someone else's formula of power can be not only dishonest but dangerous: remember the Sons of Sceva in the Acts 19 quote above. John Wimber says that he has success over demons by saying, "In the name of Jesus, I rebuke you, Evil Spirit," and zippy-whoosh there they go. Mark Bubeck simply exercises his authority that comes from his union with Jesus, and all strangleholds are broken.[8] But remember this, we do not have such a pat representation for "binding Satan" anywhere in the Bible. Paul does not once say, "Satan, I bind you." Nor does Jesus for that matter.

This "Come-out-of-her-you-dog-of-hell" liturgy seems more likely to have devolved from religious cable television.

John MacArthur warns us against becoming too enamored with our own spiritual clout. We can develop a "confrontational mentality."[9] Dr. Peter Masters agrees. He wrote: "What a triumph for the devil if he can take away the faith of true Christian people so that instead of grounding their hope on what God has said, they come to depend on a constant flow of visible proofs saying, 'I must see amazing signs and wonders!'"[10] It is always dangerous to have a "Wow!" based faith. In the first place, the "wows" have to get continually bigger to keep impressing those addicted to spiritual experience rather than scriptural evidence. Second, this experientially based lifestyle spirals ever downward into pits of brinkmanship where believers are prone to say, "My demons were bigger than your demons!"

Ultimate Triumph

For God did not give us a spirit of timidity, but a spirit of power, of love and of self-discipline.

2 TIMOTHY 1:7

Regarding our enemy we have Christ's own special promises. First, he promised us that the "gates of Hell" would not prevail against his church (Matthew 16:18). Second, he gave us a specific promise regarding the dark world of the demonic: "I have given you authority to trample on snakes and scorpions and to overcome all the power of the enemy; nothing will harm you" (Luke 10:19). From the additional material in Mark come these words as well: "And these signs will accompany those who believe: In my name they will drive out demons; . . . they will pick up snakes with their hands; and when they drink deadly poison, it will not hurt them at all" (Mark 16:17–18).

Paul likewise promised us in Romans 8:38–39, "For I am convinced that neither death nor life, neither angels nor demons, neither the present nor the future, nor any powers, neither height nor depth, nor anything else in all creation, will be able to separate us from the love of God that is in Christ Jesus our Lord." The Scriptures again and again become our unfailing confidence in our victory over all of these furious creatures of hell.

Martin Luther wrote of this victory as well:

And though this world with devils filled,
should threaten to undo us,
We will not fear for God hath willed,
His truth to triumph through us:
The Prince of Darkness grim,
We tremble not for him;
His rage we can endure,
For lo, his doom is sure,
One little word shall fell him.

("A MIGHTY FORTRESS IS OUR GOD")

Our confidence need not suffer even in the congress of the demonic. We are God's overcomers—the people whose confidence is not rooted in their own strength but in the strength of him who indwells us.

Eighteenth-century French mystic Madame Guyon wrote of her victory over Satan:

After the accident which befell me [a fall from a horse] from which I soon wonderfully recovered, the Devil began to declare himself more openly mine enemy, to break loose and become outrageous. One night, when I least thought of it, something very monstrous and frightful presented itself. It seemed a kind face, which was seen by a glimmering bluish light. I don't know whether the flame itself composed that horrible face or appearance; for it was so mixed and passed by so rapidly, that I could not discern it. My soul rested in its calm situation and assurance, and it appeared no more after that manner. As I arose at midnight to pray, I heard frightful noises in my chamber and after I had lain down they were still worse. My bed often shook for a quarter of an hour at a time, and the sashes were all burst. Every morning while this continued, they were found shattered and torn, yet I felt no fear. I arose and lighted my wax candle at a lamp which I kept in my room, because I had taken the office of sacristan and the care of waking the sisters at the hour they were to rise, without having once failed in it for my indispositions, ever being the first in all the observances. I made use of my little light to look all over the room and at the sashes, at the very time the noise was strongest. As he saw that I was afraid of nothing, he left off all on a sudden, and attacked me no more in person.[11]

We have Christ's promise of presence when the very appearance of Satan makes us afraid.

Once while lecturing to a large student gathering in Mississippi, I felt this old, familiar, bone-chilling terror. At the end of my lecture, a group of young people brought to me a young man who, to every evidence, was a most tortured soul. His eyes were turned up inside their sockets so that none of the color was showing, giving him a most eerie appearance. His limbs were terribly trembling. His body was as rigid as those of anyone in *grand mal* seizure, though those who brought him in assured me he was not epileptic. While several students restrained his sporadic wild thrashings, we began to pray for this violent young man. While we prayed over him I noticed he was wearing a New-Age crystal amulet around his neck. As I demanded that Satan free the boy, I tore the amulet from his neck. I have never seen myself as an exorcist and only on a few occasions had I ever used such an exorcism formula. Still, at my words—upon the instant that I tore the amulet from his neck—his body relaxed. In a matter of seconds he became lucid and most genial.

What amazes me even still is that I found myself most afraid of whatever was filling the young man with such obvious tension and desperation. When I thought it through later, I wondered why I was surprised. I had only acted out Jesus' promise of Luke 10:19—that he would give all believers the right to be free of the reign of Satan; indeed, we have power over the enemy in his name. I had merely discovered Christ's great power available to all Christians who are willing to claim the truth: "Greater is he that is in you than he that is in the world."

Conclusion

The weapons we fight with are not the weapons of the world. On the contrary, they have divine power to demolish strongholds.

2 CORINTHIANS 10:4

The final three chapters of this book will deal with some of those areas in which you must engage in spiritual combat. Your Christian warfare will be fought in only three areas: money, sex, and power. Each of these areas may be unpresuming places where you will meet Satan so subtly you will not be aware he is there. If you want to win over Satan, you need to remember five things. First, to conquer him you must have some overcoming strategy. In every area of your triumph, your pilgrimage will pass through the simple, dark geography of territories that seem threatening. But however frightening your spiritual struggle appears, do not let their terrors confuse you. Learn your areas of personal weaknesses. Mark them clearly as places where you are likely to encounter the devil. Then you can eliminate those threatening circumstances that ever lure you into giving the devil some little foothold (Ephesians 4:27), so that he may sift you as wheat (Luke 22:31).

Second, you need to remember that ego lies at the basis of most every temptation. At the low shrine of ego we lose all interest in Christ's call to self-denial and begin to ask, "What's in this for me?" This simple question is the mark of human lostness. It reveals our temptation to worship the self. Christ's altar is never a shrine to ego. The discipline his altar summons from us is our only safeguard against the more accessible altars of our tempter.

A third thing you need to remember is that secret sins, unconfessed, give Satan the edge in all spiritual warfare. Lilith, the night hag, is mentioned only once in the Bible (Isaiah 34:14). She proves all that Isaiah has in mind for this dark demonic enticer. She seems to be set forth as the keeper of all you would like to keep hidden from God and your family and friends. She is always there, as regular as night itself, tempting you to believe that she will keep secret what you must keep hidden lest it destroy you. She is the goddess of the moral shadows, making you believe you can get by with almost anything. Her covert temptation to you is to do what you will and hide it beneath her skirts. With such dark beginnings she will lure you to the indulgence of all appetite. Lilith will always be there, waiting for you at the end of the long day. She will always be on the next stool at the bar or under the canopy of a dimly lit lounge. Do not try to exorcise her by showing her pictures of your family in the hotel room. She will not care about them. Do not try to push her from your lap, nor ignore her illegal, and embezzling schemes for your profit-sharing plans. Lilith will trick you, promising to keep all the secrets you tell her, while all the time revealing your libertinism. She is the goddess of blackmail, determined to expose you and laugh at your spiritual impotence and final destruction. Hear her, as Ulysses' men once heard the sirens that summoned his sailors to death. For in the temptation of getting by without getting caught, presidents have known impeachment and clergymen have sullied their character to the point that their ministries were lost forever.

How well Jesus counseled us in this matter: "There is nothing concealed that will not be disclosed, or hidden that will not be made known. What you have said in the dark will be heard in the daylight, and what you have whispered in the ear in the inner rooms will be proclaimed from the roofs" (Luke 12:2–3).

There is not the slightest possibility of your getting by with that which you commit to the secret keeping of Lilith, the night hag.

The fourth thing you must remember is that Satan is the nomadic nightstalker. Away from home you will meet the tempter who is always wandering up and down throughout the earth (Job 1:7), seeking whom he may devour (1 Peter 5:8). He is the vagabond tempter, the celestial wanderer who will enjoy meeting you in that land far from home where things take longer to be seen and reported. His is the temptation that comes from beyond the country where we are known and recognized. His is the demon's domain, where we presume ourselves free from recognition. He often travels with Lilith the seductress of every family value. Satan teaches us to desire away from home what would seem unlikely ever to be discovered by those we have left behind.

Never forget this: when Satan was cast out of heaven, he realized he was a being without a country of his own. Except for his terminal dungeon of the abyss, he is homeless in the earth. Jude pictured the errant satanic teachers of his day as wandering stars (Jude 13), erratic and deceptive in their allurement and destruction. Beware every thought that you can escape the moral requirements of God in some remote place. These homeless demons know your travel plans. Those who leave their fee on the nightstands find that the pictures of their family never mean so much again. They find that they never can go home again.

Finally, you must never forget that just as God is the Creator, who made you and wants to make your life and testimony beautiful, Satan is the Destroyer. He is called Abaddon in the Old Testament and Apollyon in the New. He is out to smash every beautiful thing that God created you to be and to achieve. Satan exists to see that you never come to realize your full potential as a believer in Christ. He is not the "wrecker-ball" destroyer whose destruction of your life is huge and obvious. He is the lord of the termites, whose unseen decay makes Pharisees seem alive when they are only the hollow dead.

The destroyer will harass you unless you take him seriously. All that you have built can be smashed in a single instance of poor allegiance to Christ (1 Corinthians 10:10). He rarely comes to us asking us to sign a contract for our souls. He is rather the god of side deals, who never buys souls all at once. He purchases us on the installment plan. As God gains great delight from creating the beautiful, so Satan gets his delights from destroying the beautiful life and crushing the steadfast commitment.

With these five reminders, let us now venture into the three arenas of our warfare: money, sex, and power. You will deal with these great, demonic foes all your life. But, do not despair at the size of these enemies. They are not so formidable as you may think. Christ did the heavy work of your warfare two thousand years ago when he hung by his hands to show you the clear course of your struggle. He won. Do not despair. You will too.

3

THE RUMOR
OF VICTORY

*When you were dead in your sins and in the
uncircumcision of your sinful nature, God made
you alive with Christ.... And having disarmed the
powers and authorities, he made a public spectacle
of them, triumphing over them by the cross.*

COLOSSIANS 2:13, 15

He laid hold on the dragon, that old serpent ...

REVELATION 20:2 (KJV)

In his book *People of the Lie*, popular psychiatrist and writer M. Scott Peck records various incidents that he considered demonic. He even admits to participating in exorcisms. In one dark instance, he tells of a young man who committed suicide with a rifle. The next Christmas, the father of the suicide gave his surviving son that very rifle for a Christmas present. Shortly after that Christmas, Peck was chosen as the psychiatrist to counsel and treat the surviving son with psychotherapy. Peck confesses that when the boy was brought to him for counsel he had literally picked sores all over his face and hands (such picking is an indication of self-destructive tendencies, says Peck).[1] The popular psychiatrist confesses that such cases reflect the presence of personal evil in the center of many psychotic relationships.

People of every of race and clime have some moral code. This code generally comes from a belief in some god, which they see as the source of good. Along with this good god they also believe in some kind of evil god or spirit. The Loki of the Norse pantheon is the Pluto of the Roman pantheon is the Sipapu monster of the Anasazi is the Voo Doo of Haiti is the Pazuzu of ancient Assyria. This evil force is known by some name in virtually every world religion.

In the Bible this evil power is called Satan. He exists only as a foe weakened by his own defeat. Christians can see him in only one way: thrown out of heaven and waiting his final judgment. His future is hopelessly reserved in chains forever (Revelation 20:2,10). This image of our enemy's defeat, like faith itself, we cannot prove. Just as trust is the essence of our salvation, we must trust God's report in Scripture. Therefore, while our spiritual struggle of the moment may be serious, it is only for the moment. The fact of the cross and resurrection are history—finished, written, and recorded. We may trust it. Yet we serve it as the grand rumor, which while certain to come true has not yet come to us. It is not a rumor to be tried but one to be demonstrated as we work toward its fulfillment. We are the owners of a confident rumor: Satan is beaten. Already vanquished. Our joyous advantage lies in knowing it is the confident end of our story. Throughout the history of the church, Christian art has pictured our ultimate victory. Our confidence is substantiated in sculpture and on canvas. Satan is pictured as the dragon beneath the heel of Michael. He is seen as the leathery and horned demiurge of Michaelangelo's last judgment, already bound in chains.

In spite of this rumor of victory, history has been marked by our human fascination with evil. When the Nazis came to power in Germany, demonic occurrences and societies began to flourish. Secular novelists have built reader tension by describing the devil as more formidable than he is. Take Ira Levin's best-seller in which the devil proclaims the birth of *Rosemary's Baby.*

We are so intrigued by the devil we tend to paint him with more power than he actually has. We fascinate ourselves with hellish Frankensteins that we portray in film and novel as unbeatable. How false! To counter these mistaken notions, we need to read the Scriptures until we are convinced of our victory. Only then we will be able to see the devil in proper proportion. Then we will recognize his strategy of perpetrating evil through ordinary human relationships rather than extraordinary phenomena.

There is another way the devil harasses us. Whenever we try to pry the future out of God's hand the devil is present. We are tempted by crystal balls, palm readers, and mediums, all to find out from Satan what God will not reveal to us more than one day at a time.

The late Bishop Pike offers a case in point. Early in his career he jettisoned what he considered to "the bulky biblical doctrines" of the Virgin Birth and Resurrection. After his son, Jim, committed suicide, Pike became involved in a bizarre round of seances, trying to contact his son's departed spirit. He appeared to be carrying a great deal of guilt for his son's suicide. A Canadian medium "established contact" with a spirit that at last pronounced Pike's absolution. The bishop felt better at receiving spiritual absolution "from the other side," though he never seemed to be himself after dabbling with spiritualists and mediums. "Feeling unfulfilled," he went to Israel seeking a deeper spiritual fulfillment that eluded him. He seemed locked inside himself. Finally, preoccupied, remote, and somehow out of touch with reality, he disappeared. After some time, his dead body was found in the desert wearing only cotton briefs. In trying to pry the unknown from the grip of God, his own life was taken from him in hidden circumstances we cannot even guess. The horror of this utter tragedy is that Pike could not accept the "rumor of victory," trusting that Christ had triumphed and he had won. The power of Christ's victory was lost to him since he felt no need to depend upon that triumph. Unlike Pike, we must appropriate the conquering work of Christ to be victorious ourselves. Pike proved that as real as Christ's victory is, it cannot impart its power to those who will not trust it.

But how do we proceed with our own warfare? We are to begin with the confidence that the war is already won and that our ultimate home is heaven, a place our enemy can never enter. We are to proceed on the powerful rumor of victory, a rumor which must not allow us to consider our foe trivial. Though trivial to God, Satan is not trivial. Having been beaten by God, he can only be beaten by us when we fully understand how we must fight. Our tactics are three: first, we must "name the powers"; second, we must avoid the hidden or the *occult* in favor of the revealed; and third, we must fully accept the rumor of victory, just as we earlier trusted in Christ to save and sanctify us.

Naming the Powers

If you ask anything in my name, I will do it.
JOHN 16:23 (RSV)

The primary tactic of our warfare involves the naming of the powers. But who are they and what are the specific advantages of naming them? Paul talks about naming the powers in the book of Ephesians. Written to the Christians at Ephesus, Paul's letter was addressed to those who had come to follow Christ in a city known for its worship of magical powers. These powers were seen by ancients as malevolent forces that could be put to use by those who knew how to get in touch with them. The only way to have control over these forces was to be able to name the various powers the magician or warlock was using against you. To know the name of a particular demon or evil power was to hold a kind of control over it.

So often in the New Testament exorcisms are a name-calling battle:

Mark 5:9: "My name is Legion," says the demoniac to Jesus, and once having his *name* Jesus could cast him out.

Mark 16:17: "In my name they will drive out demons," said Jesus in his farewell to his disciples from the Mount of Ascension.

Ephesians 1:21 (RSV) alleges that God gave Jesus, in the resurrection, a place "far above all principality, and power, and might, and dominion, and every name that is named, not only in this world, but also in that which is to come."

Philippians 2:9–10 alleges that "God exalted him to the highest place and gave him the name that is above every name, that at the name of Jesus every knee should bow, in heaven and on earth and under the earth."

Acts 19:13–16 records, "Some Jews who went around driving out evil spirits tried to invoke the name of the Lord

Jesus over those who were demon-possessed. They would say, 'In the name of Jesus, whom Paul preaches, I command you to come out.' ... One day, the evil spirit answered them, 'Jesus I know, and I know about Paul, but who are you?" Then the man who had the evil spirit jumped on them and overpowered them all. He gave them such a beating that they ran out of the house naked and bleeding." It is important that you use the strong *name* of God (that is, Jesus) if you are going to overcome the weaker powers.

The Hebrew word for "name" is *shem* and the Greek word is *onoma*. In biblical literature the name of God stood for God himself and as such was to be revered by commandment, the third commandment (Exodus 20:7). To merely speak the name of God was somehow to overthrow evil or effect the work of salvation. The *shem Yahweh*, or "the name of Yahweh," was considered to be identical with Yahweh himself. If God was not to be considered lightly, then neither was his name. Psalm 54:1 one reads (in the Septuagint), "Save me, O God, by thy name (*onoma*) ..."[2] Hebrews often coupled the name *El*, for God, with many compound forms such as *El-Shaddai* ("God Almighty") or *Elijah* ("The Lord is God"). If such evidence of the power of the divine name needs reinforcement, consider the fact that God shared the power of his name. All Old Testament words that combine with "El," or God, are words that link the power of God to the name with which they are attached. Consider the names of the ruler angels or archangels: Michael, Gabriel, Uriel, Azael, etc.[3]

As a word of power, *onoma*, or name, is used 226 times in the New Testament and 97 of those times it refers to Jesus as Christ or as Lord. Only 7 of those times does the word refer to the satanic name. But only of the name of Jesus does the New Testament say he was given a name that is above every name (Philippians 2:11).[4]

Paul names these powers in Ephesians 1:21 with three Greek words. Thomas B. White breaks down these demonic powers using Paul's terms but calling them the officers of "Hell's Corporate Headquarters":

> Paul brings light to the topic by depicting the powers as organized in a hierarchy of rulers/principalities (*archai*), authorities (*exousia*), powers (*dunamis*), and spiritual forces of evil (*kosmokratoras*). It is reasonable to assume that the authority structure here is arranged in descending order. Daniel 10:13 and 20 unveil the identity of the *archai* as high level satanic princes set over nations and regions of the earth. The word *exousia* carries a connotation of both supernatural and natural government. In the Apostle's understanding, there were supernatural forces that stood behind human structures. Paul no doubt is voicing the Jewish apocalyptic notion of cosmic beings who were given authority by God to arbitrate human affairs. Presumably, the *dunamis* operate within countries and cultures to influence certain aspects of life. The *krasmokratoras* are the many types of evil spirits that commonly afflict ordinary people, e.g., spirits of deception, divination, lust, rebellion, fear and infirmity. These, generally, are the evil powers confronted and cast out in most deliverance sessions.[5]

The names of all these various kinds of powers employed in Ephesians, chapter one, were essential to the success of diviners and magicians. Dr. Clint Arnold, to whom I owe so much of my understanding in this area, offers this insight: the calling of the names of the supernatural "powers" was fundamental to the practice of magic. The ancient Ephesians had an occult confidence in six special, magical names. They knew how to use these "names of power" for their own advancement through life. They carried those names on inscribed amulets, cameos, or gems. Repeating those names was essential for enlisting the help of the demons that the amulets signified. This was the essence of magic.[6] Sometimes magicians carried the written names of the demons by which exorcists cast out other demons on their bodies in phylacteries. The very wearing of their names gave the magicians power over other less powerful demons.[7]

However one names the powers, the occult world must always be confronted in this way. Demons have almost always been summoned by name and where they are named, the exorcism ritual becomes all powerful and uncontested. Where they are not summoned by name or summoned only in a weak name (see the Sons of Sceva passage in Acts 19) they are rarely cast out.

What then are we to take for the meaning of all this naming of the powers in order to have authority over areas of demons or weakness? Just this: deal with God frankly and openly, unashamedly naming the problem areas of your life, and in this you will be able to so thoroughly resist the devil that he will flee from you (James 4:7). Practically this "naming of your problem area" works the same way that confession works. Remember that 1 John 1:9 says, "If we confess our sins, he is faithful and just and will forgive us our sins and purify us from all unrighteousness." The word "confess" here comes from the Greek *homologeo,* which means "to admit" or "own up to."

No real inner healing can come to those who will not admit the evil that proceeds from their lives. In the same way, God cannot fortify us against the advances of Satan until we acknowledge those areas of our vulnerability. Remember this: we have power over our weaknesses as we are willing to own up to them. Our victory over the evil one is made possible as we specifically confront him in the power of the name of Jesus, the name that is above all names. To name in this manner is to refuse to give the devil entrance to your life (Ephesians 4:27). Victory lies in knowing the name and size and battle tactics of your enemy. As Christ said, "Suppose a king is about to go to war against another king. Will he not first sit down and consider whether he is able with ten thousand men to oppose the one coming against him with twenty thousand?" (Luke 14:31). Knowing the size of your enemy and using the name of Jesus is your certain deliverance. There is no other name under heaven given among human beings whereby we must be saved (Acts 4:12).

The Hidden Things of Darkness

There is nothing concealed that will not be disclosed, or hidden that will not be made known.

MATTHEW 10:26

Therefore judge nothing before the appointed time; wait till the Lord comes. He will bring to light what is hidden in darkness and will expose the motives in men's hearts.

1 CORINTHIANS 4:5

The second tactic of our warfare is an agreement that we will make with ourselves. We must agree that we will avoid every kind of evil (1 Thessalonians 5:22), always abhorring all that is set against God (Romans 12:9). As we have said, one of the most powerful words for God is

Creator, and this word is always in contrast to one of the most powerful words for Satan, the *Destroyer.* Just so, one of the most powerful words that capture God's behavior toward us is *apocalupsis,* or revelation. As you would expect, there is an opposite word that describes Satan: *occultus,* a Latin word meaning *hidden.* God reveals, Satan conceals. God's power is always open: his miracles come in full light. Satan on the other hand loves the night. There his demoralizing deeds work horrors—there where light is thin and gloom clots hope.

Darkness is the province of evil. Demons do not declare themselves.

Satan has great power but it operates covertly and in darkness. Hence he is called the "ruler of darkness" (Ephesians 6:12). But the Bible says that in Christ there is no darkness at all (1 John 1:5); indeed Jesus called himself the light (John 12:46), and the Apostle said that all who followed him were the sons of light (1 Thessalonians 5:5).

One of the chief ways that we give place to the devil (Ephesians 4:27) is that desire we all have to know the future ahead of time. We could all do a lot better planning if we could drag the future from its shadowy hiddenness into the glaring light of the "right now." If we could only do this, we would be a lot more secure and we would have ultimate control over those who couldn't do it. Security and power would ultimately belong to those who keep tomorrow in their pockets. With most the desire is committed unto God and left there. But not with all. Many traffic with the forces of darkness to try and know this great unknowable.

There are many ways to dabble in the occult. The first is what the Bible calls a spirit of divination. This kind of spirit was evident in Acts 16:16, which describes a young girl who follows Paul along the street crying out against him. The spirit of divination, apparently a demon, enabled the girl to "tell fortunes." In short, these spirits were summoned up to tell the future. Even today there are many ways to go about this. Much of the witches' movement in our time seems to be an attempt to wrest from these exotic and demonic creatures special insight into the future. All who wish to prevent the devil from gaining standing room in their lives should keep away from witches and the counsel they purport to offer. Vain is their promise to pry the heavy lid off the future to give us a peek inside.

This would certainly be true of either the white- or the black-witch movement. White witches seem to have a better reputation than their counterparts. But beware! A witch of any color is a witch too far. Sybil Leek, a British white witch, some years ago assured both Americans and Brits that they had nothing to fear in trusting the magic of white witches. For, she contended, while black witches performed evil deeds, white witches only used their magic to do good deeds like getting people jobs and healing the sick. Unlike the gruesome killing and fecal-and-blood rituals of black witches, white-witch gatherings were often elegant coven affairs ending with ice-cream and cake.[8]

Witches have haunted both American and European literature. Nathaniel Hawthorne's *Young Goodman Brown* deals with a black mass, which a young Massachusetts churchman discovers on his way home from a town meeting. *The Crucible* by Arthur Miller is an excellent play telling the tale of New England witchery. John Updike's *Witches of Eastwick* does the same. The consecration of altars for black masses has long been a subject of horror and intrigue, in which crucifixes are smeared with human excrement and the Lord's prayer is recited backwards.

Why would anyone endure these ghastly nocturnals? The truth is that many would rather risk some dark trafficking of their souls rather than be kept in ignorance about the future. Macbeth, for instance, consults with the hags in Shakespeare's play to gain some insight into how his dubious reign is going to turn out. Shakespeare apparently realized that those who deal in the black arts do it to have a secure future. But all who trust witches betray true trust. Paul would back Shakespeare. Those with spirits of divination are those who have seducing spirits. "The Spirit clearly says that in later times some will abandon the faith and follow deceiving spirits and things taught by demons" (1 Timothy 4:1).

Kurt Koch called this kind of evil witchery a gathering of Satan's elite troops.[9]

This kind of gathering may be summoned by a seance. King Saul of Israel, while publicly decrying the use of witches and mediums (1 Samuel 28:3), is at last so troubled about his own future and his desire to know the outcome of the pending battle of Mount Gilboa, he cries, "Find me a woman who is a medium, so I may go to her and inquire of her" (1 Samuel 28:7). In a private seance he unhappily forces the woman to summon the shade of the old prophet Samuel. The spirit of Samuel does reveal his future:

> Samuel said to Saul, "Why have you disturbed me by bringing me up?"
> "I am in great distress," Saul said. "The Philistines are fighting against me, and God has turned away from me. He no longer answers me, either by prophets or by

dreams. So I have called on you to tell me what to do."
(1 Samuel 28:15)

Then the shade of Samuel reveals Saul's unhappy future: "The Lord will hand over both Israel and you to the Philistines, and tomorrow you and your sons will be with me" (1 Samuel 28:19).

No witch is ever a happy source of truth.

So perhaps the question needs to be, "When are you dabbling in the occult?" Anytime you have an unwholesome desire to know the safest course to pursue into the future? It may begin in such a simple thing as being concerned over stock-options, investment counseling, or job changes. But however minimal the desire seems, it can bring up an unholy desire. The best course is to deal quickly and firmly with the desire, entrusting the future to God.

There are many other more usual kinds of dabbling in the occult. Some of these ways involve palm reading or tarot cards, which first appeared in Europe at the beginning of the fourteenth century. Remember at the center of Blatty's very popular novel was a Ouija board. The word *Ouija* was formed by uniting the French and German words for *yes*. These devices came into production at the end of the nineteenth century and focused on a planchette that moved on felt across an ebony board pointing out letters to spell out lengthy answers or the words *yes* or *no* providing shorter answers to user's requests.

Perhaps the most popular way to dabble in the occult involves astrology. Moses some 3400 years ago wrote: "And when you look up to the sky and see the sun, the moon and the stars—all the heavenly array—do not be enticed into bowing down to them and worshiping . . ." (Deuteronomy 4:19).

There is a further mention of just how abominable these stargazers were: "If a man or woman living among you . . . has worshipped other gods, bowing down to them or to the sun or the moon or the stars of the sky, . . . stone that person to death" (Deuteronomy 17:2–5).

God specifically commands his church not to be involved with astrology, and to do it is to go against God and to "give the devil a foothold" (Ephesians 4:27).

Remember, as the word *occultus* means "hidden," the word *apocalupsis* (apocalypse) is where we get the word for *revelation*. It is Satan's nature to act in hiddenness. But God's word *apocalypse,* or *revelation,* means "to bring out of hiddenness." Apocalypse is essentially a word for drawing back the curtain to let us see what is hidden behind it. It is our nature to think of Revelation as that book of the Bible that focuses on those hidden things that will come at the end of time. But the real idea of Revelation is much bigger than that. It is essentially a word that means "to draw what is hidden into openness or disclosure."

Since the beginning of God's love affair with the human race, he has chosen to let us know who he is. In other words he has revealed himself to us. God's revelation, or self-disclosure, means that we cannot pull God out of his hiddenness. Instead, he actively reveals himself in the world. Though we do not yet see him face to face, he beckons to us, saying, "Here I am" in nature—in the dewy rose or the glistening mountain peak. He says, "Here I am" in the glory of human loving, for never are we more like God than when we love. But when he wanted to say, "Here I am" in full disclosure, he came in Jesus. So fully was God revealed in Christ, that Jesus said, "Anyone who has seen me has seen the Father" (John 14:9), and, "I and the Father are one" (John 10:30).

Many years ago Hollywood made a film depicting the story of Will Rogers' life. The director wanted to find an actor who had all of Rogers' wit, coy grin, and mannerisms. Naturally, he picked Will Rogers Jr. Those who wanted to see the father need look only at the son. The son, down to the very genes and chromosomes, *was* his father.

When God wanted to show us the fullest revelation of himself he stepped from glory into a manger at Bethlehem. Then at last, the child's question, "Mommy, what does God look like?" was answered. For Jesus was God's fullest revelation of himself. Now when that which is hidden makes you afraid, you need only draw open the drapes. Let the sunlight of God's utter love fall on Satan's hiddenness. His light will dispel the darkness within and around you. The occult is no match for the one who Reveals. Satan has been judged. In the very midst of hell, God says loudly, "Here I Am! Be gone you terrifying devils. This is my child!"

Jesus made it clear that God's self-declaring righteousness would always be characterized by the light. "I am the light," he said (John 8:12). Jesus earlier said that John the Baptist was not that light, only its witness. Jesus is "the true light that gives light to every man . . . coming into the world" (John 1:9). But the most uncompromising division by which Jesus distinguishes the darkness and light is this: "Light has come into the world, but men loved darkness instead of light because their deeds were evil. Everyone who does evil hates the light, and will not come into the light for fear that his deeds will be exposed" (John 3:19–20).

The Rumor of Defeat

How you have fallen from heaven,
O morning star, son of the dawn!
You have been cast down to earth,
you who once laid low the nations! ...
Those who see you stare at you,
they ponder your fate:
"Is this the man who shook the earth
and made kingdoms tremble ... ?"

ISAIAH 14:12,16

The link in the chain of victory over Satan involves accepting the rumor of Satan's defeat. Why would I use the word *rumor*? Why would I not simply say the *fact* of Satan's defeat. Because we are still dealing in the area of faith. I trust a Christ whom I have never seen with my physical eyes. I believe that this yet-to-be-seen Christ has defeated the devil. Yet I live in the confidence of something I cannot prove to unbelievers: this rumor, I do indeed trust as a fact. It is the trusting that gives Christ's victory real force in my life. Satan's threat to all of us was over the moment that our wounded Savior looked into the heavens and cried "*It is finished!*" (John 19:30). This was the final turn of the screw by which the enemy was forever barred from heaven. But more than this, in that cry from the cross, evil was prohibited from ever being eternally effective in the lives of God's children. There exists all about us the rumor of Satan's defeat. He has been judged and banished from heaven. He can never enter that wonderful finality which will be our home forever.

The issue of our successful warfare is crystallized in two simple questions: how and why? Whenever we think of Satan in any of the contexts mentioned above, we think of "how?" When we think of Houdini or any of the more contemporary illusionists we are forever asking "how?" How do they do what they do? With such a small three letter word we are forever trying to bludgeon our way into the hidden and the unknown.

But as we mature in Christ we gradually abandon our fascination with the celestial mechanics of "how." Sweltering under the mystery of our salvation we lose all interest in how God splits the sea, or raises the dead. God is, after all, God. He is not accustomed to explaining himself. Even if he did, we would not have the excellence of wit to understand him. Satan has never understood God either. Indeed he cannot. But God completely understands Satan. For the maker always understands that which he makes. Satan is in exile, baffled by the mysteries of him whose throne he would have taken. He was cast out of heaven trying to figure out "how" to lift his throne above the stars of God. With the Cross he lost every hope of controlling God's children except by those who willingly give him their own consent.

But if we do not ask *how* it is that God does a thing, what is it we may ask? We may ask "why?" Why would God, so all-complete in himself, ever stop to consider our lostness? The question is splendidly reckoned in Anselm's great book *Cur Deus Homo?*—"Why did God become a human being?" Anselm gives his magnificent answer in a single word: *grace*. It is only because God loved, with a love past all explaining, that Jesus came. We can have no satisfaction to this "why" unless we reckon it totally in terms of grace.

Jerome in translating his Vulgate Bible, had no answer. But he did offer us this wonderful light: Jesus came to fully show us God *in plenitudo temporis* (Galatians 4:4)—"when the time was right." Through grace we not only discovered this self-revealing God, we came also to discover his Christ. Would you see his power? Then you must see Jesus as Lord of the Church Triumphant. Best of all, this Jesus is also Lord of all your circumstances. Satan's attempt to destroy you eternally and defeat you temporarily has ended in defeat.

But can you see that your confidence depends upon those spiritual disciplines that forge you into God's formidable soldier? Victory, as I have stressed, will never be gained by invoking quick and easy formulas. It will only come through spiritual discipline. Defeating Satan on the cross was not easy for Jesus, and you may be sure that it will not be easy for you to defeat him in your own life. If you want strength for your daily trials, you must build yourself up in prayer and Bible reading. Prayer is the easiest thing in the world to do haphazardly and the hardest thing in the world to do well. Bible reading too is easy to do casually, but difficult to do as a systematic commitment. But only as you commit yourself to these important disciplines will you develop the armor of a real soldier.

When Jesus returned from the Mount of Transfiguration, he found his disciples trying—with no success—to cast a demon out of a poor child. After Jesus had cast the demon out his disciples came to him and asked him why they had failed in their attempt to do it. Jesus answered, "Because of your unbelief . . . this kind does not go out except by prayer and fasting" (Matthew 17:20–21)."

You may have struggled for years with Satan over a particular sin. You may be the captive of some abuse that

81

will not let you go. It may be a sin of heart-darkness, where you too willingly let the evil one into your life. Please hear Jesus' words, "there are some enslavement's that will not be broken except by long seasons of prayer and fasting."

A particular evangelist of my acquaintance had an abusive, alcoholic father. The younger brother of this evangelist never ceased to pray for his Father to come to know Christ. Then one night the younger brother prayed that he would be willing to do anything to see his father come to Christ. He even agreed that he would be willing to die himself if his father could only be converted. Not long after that in a freakish car accident, the younger brother *was* killed. His father, in trying to reckon with his grief, became so needy that he at last turned to Christ. And out of such a great personal sacrifice, Satan's hold on this man was broken.

Genesis 3:15 offers the first wonderful picture of Christ, that all-powerful descendent of Adam, who will stand at last with his foot on the head of the serpent. This all glorious image of victory has given life to the church in every age. To strengthen our confidence Paul reminds us that God sees us not in terms of our struggle to win, but in terms of our finished state: "For those God foreknew he also predestined to be conformed to the likeness of his Son, that he might be the firstborn among many brothers. And those he predestined, he also called; those he called, he also justified; those he justified, he also glorified" (Romans 8:29–30). "Glorified" is that final state we shall enjoy when at last we are in the presence of the Father.

Yet this final state that we see as future, God, in his timeless eye, sees as already in effect. God sees Satan not as we see him—someday conquered—but conquered already. Michael's foot is already on the Serpent's head, and the sword of God is already raised. We won the ultimate war the very moment we came to Christ. Now all that remains for us to win are those little interim battles that shall come while we await our ultimate triumph. How have others historically won over Satan? Julian of Norwich said that Satan should be laughed out of our lives. She based this doctrine on many Old Testament passages. But there is one which is extremely poignant: "The wicked plot against the righteous and gnash their teeth at them; but the Lord laughs at the wicked, for he knows their day is coming"(Psalm 37:12–13).

Julian of Norwich knew that to laugh at anyone is to cause them ultimate pain. Derision is a powerful tool that can be used by our enemies to make us feel bad. Scorn can also be an effective spiritual tool to laugh the demons from our lives. Therefore, never underestimate the power of a cheerful spirit. Those who live continually with a cheerful spirit may well defeat Satan just by their countenance. Those demons that barter for our souls feed on depression and "poor-little-me-ism." Remember therefore that we have won the battle already. We live in a rejoicing spirit whose utter joy forces Satan out of our lives. Perhaps this is why so many of the saints rarely spoke of the devil. They lived so constantly in the power of Christ that Satan found no room to enter their hearts. Fill your own heart with genuine praise, and you will leave no room for those demons who may come to feed.

I have found one positive way to defeat the demonic realm. Learn to pray the Scriptures. This exercise is best performed by those who have learned the Scriptures. Psalm 119:11 reminds us to hide his word in our heart so we will not sin against God. What utter wisdom this is. Several times in my own life when I have been haunted by the demonic, I simply build a nest of Scriptures. Into this nest of high confidence I lay my doubts. Again and again I prove this simple truth: the nest of triumph will never hatch the eggs of hell.

If you must face some lonely moment of demonic oppression, try this little exercise. Start with the book of Genesis. Begin quoting Scriptures out loud into whatever lonely darkness is oppressing you. On one occasion when my wife and children were on a trip to see her family, our house was alone and quiet. I do not know why Satan picks such moments to make his presence felt, but that is often when he does it. On this particular evening I had been out later than usual making an important pastoral call. It was quite late and very dark when I at last stepped in through the door of our house. While I have often felt Satan's presence, until this time I had never felt it in my own home. The tempter was really there. I was not alone. In the dark just inside my doorway, I felt that subtle fear that makes the hair raise slightly on the nape of the neck. For an awful instant, I was afraid to turn on the lights. I was afraid that I might actually see this horrible presence that was oppressing me and making me afraid.

I decided not to turn on the lights at all. Instead, I dropped to my knees in the soft pile of my own carpet and began praying Scriptures. I simply started with Genesis and began quoting all the Scriptures I had memorized across the years. The minutes passed away and so did the fear. Finally, before I had prayed the Scriptures very long, I was utterly at peace and so was the house. I no longer needed to turn on the lights. After the horror came a warm enveloping darkness. Christ was all about me.

Where I had quailed before the dark fears, I now reached out in praise to a Wonderful Presence. Without any electrical illumination, I felt his wondrous inner light. Gone was the night serpent—defanged by him whose children need never fear. I slept in joy.

Conclusion

Never will I leave you; never will I forsake you.

The key to winning in spiritual warfare is to be sure you always walk with Christ. This is not a difficult thing to do, but it is highly dependent upon your use of the disciplines. Remember two things: first, there is an immense difference between demon possession and demonic oppression. My opinion is that those who are filled with Christ have not enough space in their hearts to hold Satan. You may mark it down that the indwelling Holy Spirit of God will never allow demons to live in the single domain of any human heart: "What harmony has Christ with Belial, or what has a believer in common with an unbeliever? Or what agreement has the temple of God with idols? For we are the temple of the living God; just as God said, 'I will dwell in them and walk among them; and I will be their God and they will be my people'" (2 Corinthians 6:15–16, NAS).

Both C. Fred Dickason and Merrill Unger believe that the believer cannot be owned by demons but that he may be harassed by demons.[10] But John MacArthur points out that there is not a single instance in the New Testament of any believer being demon possessed.[11]

James asks in another context: "Does a spring send forth fresh water and bitter water from the same opening?"

(James 3:11 NKJV). As has been said, what comes out of us in a crisis is what we're full of. If we are full of Christ, in the crisis we will produce good works and praise to our Redeemer. If we permit our heart to be filled with evil, then in the crisis evil and defeat will issue from our lives. Squeeze a lemon and all a lemon can give is bitterness.

But it is quite possible for any Christian to walk afar from God. Our remoteness to the Savior will permit the enemy to move in close. We are ever pursued by all kinds of evil. If evil occupies our hearts, our hearts will be captive. In such captivity we will not be able to win over temptation, and all that God wants for us will be lost. Sin comes mostly from our eager surrender to our appetites. Be sure when you give yourself to temptation you do not try to blame God for that evil that issues from your life. "Blessed is the man," says James, "who perseveres under trial, because when he has stood the test, he will receive the crown of life that God has promised to those who love him. When tempted, no one should say, 'God is tempting me.' For God cannot be tempted by evil, nor does he tempt anyone; but each one is tempted when, by his own evil desire, he is dragged away and enticed" (James 1:12–14). If you walk with Satan your fruit will be satanic. If with God, godly. Do not think you will barter evil for advance and then at last switch to the good. Evil is so gently narcotic that it gains our souls by inches yet holds us through eternity.

Could it be that the rich man who lifted up his eyes in hell begging Lazarus to dip his finger in the water and cool his tongue was a man lost in his own narcotic greed? Perhaps he always intended to reform. Someday he believed he would be generous. At last he would live like God. Alas, his lifetime of immoral side-deals could not produce a dram of godliness. Usually we die cherishing all that we cherished while we were in better health. We cannot use darkness to get ahead in life and then suddenly cherish light.

In *Dr. Faustus*, it is fitting that the hero is dragged at last into hell. Hell was his constant stream of choices. It is inconsistent that in his final moments his whole-hearted service of Satan should reverse itself. Can Hitler in his dying moments repent and bless the Jews, come to Christ, and beg the world's forgiveness for the war that cost a hundred million souls? Can those who forever sold free men into slavery be soon forgiven as though their sins were naught? I speak not to disparage deathbed conversions. It is good to come to Christ at any moment, but the flow of our moral choices becomes habitual. Both our sins and deeds of righteousness are ritually made. We seldom break those evil rituals of choosing in our final moments to embrace the Christ, we should have made our captain years ago.

What is our odd service of Satan all about? What motivates it? Why do we begin to worship at Lucifer's low altar? We do so because we are usually looking for those special bargains of ego that advance us into the world we so want to control. We are captive to the age-old common indulgences of money, sex, and power. This trinity of demons in one way or another controls us so completely that the shinier reality of grace is lost.

I well remember an old man who had come to Christ only in his latter days. At his dying he told me how grateful he was that at last he belonged to Christ. But he lamented, "I have spent a lifetime loving all the wrong things. I spent my life making good deals and amassed what seemed a secure future. Yet here on the brink of eternity, I can see now it was a pittance. Oh, that I had been as interested in serving Christ as I was in making good deals."

Satan is the lord of the good deal. But the good deal is based only on what is good for us. Hell is filled with those who spent their lives looking for good deals. In the purchase of each one of them, a little more of their soul is chained. At last, they themselves are inseparable from their bargain purchases. We are swiftly sold Satan, while all the time we think we are merely getting on in life. Our appetites are the coins with which we buy eternity. If we hunger for Christ we will own both this life and the next. To make deals is to own neither. To love God and serve the rumor of victory may be a matter of singing with confidence in the valley of death. In such a gentle song we will lose our need to shout, "Get thee behind me, Satan!" Instead, our melody will drive away the creatures of fury. The song of the conquerors is the gentle exorcism of our confidence:

> *My Jesus I love thee, I know thou art mine.*
> *For thee all the follies of sin I resign.*
> *My gracious Redeemer. My Savior art thou.*
> *If ever I loved Thee, my Jesus 'tis now.*
> WILLIAM J. FEATHERSTON (1846–1873)

Two

NAMING THE
POWERS

4

MAMMON: THE MONEY DEMON

May your money perish with you, because you
thought you could buy the gift of God with money!
(SIMON PETER TO SIMON THE SORCERER) ACTS 8:20

ylvester was a poor brother of the new order of Francis of Assisi. On one occasion he saw Francis giving money to the poor and was instantly overcome with greed. He rebuked Francis by reminding him of a long-unpaid debt: "You never paid me for all the stones you took to repair the churches."

Francis reached into the money bag and pulled out a double handful and dumped it overflowing into Sylvester's hands. Sylvester went home and gloated over his money. Then he began to feel ashamed of his greed. For three nights Sylvester had a special revelation from God, telling him that in spite of the money he took from Francis, it was Francis who had true wealth. Sylvester's heart was crushed, and he repented of his greed. Once he gave up his lust for money, the demonic force of its glitter was gone from his life. How wise we are when we seek wealth of the Spirit, which looses Satan's stranglehold on our lives.[1]

I own an antique violin. Late one night I was entertaining a group of friends, one of whom was a violinist in the Omaha Symphony. Spotting the instrument, he became excited. "Do you know the history of this piece?" he asked. I did not.

"Do you have a flashlight?" he then asked.

"Of course," I replied, going off to fetch it.

When shining the flashlight through the curled cuts on the front of the instrument I discovered the words "CREMONA ITALY, 1712 FACIEBAT, ANTONIO STRADI-VARI." I was stunned! The violin had come to me from my wife's grandfather, who had bought it used and had no idea where it had come from. For years it had hung on my wall in a collage of musical instruments just over the piano. But now all was changed. I had discovered those glorious Latin words. I had a genuine Stradivarius.

I am not proud of how I felt after I discovered the inscription. My whole demeanor changed. I decided that I shouldn't keep the violin at home. I thought I should place it in a bank vault and to seek legal council on how to hide it from grandpa's other "greedy" grandchildren who would now be incensed that I had his $300,000 violin. I determined to keep the matter hidden until I could sell it and buy a new Mercedes and a river front home. I began to think how I would have to be firm and perhaps ugly with the other heirs—in a sweet Christian spirit, of course—in case it became necessary for me to stand up to them in court. I ultimately became inwardly callused in defending my new wealth.

Then I had the demonic antique evaluated. It was a forgery. Essentially worthless.

I was ashamed but deliciously liberated from the clutches of the great monster greed. But the best and worst thing about coming to my senses was that I realized I had not behaved like Jesus. Then I took a further step of spiritual honesty: I admitted I had been serving the demon Mammon.

The Great Either-Or

You cannot serve God and mammon.

MATTHEW 6:24 (RSV)

Mammon is an old Aramaic word, probably older than coined money itself, which properly means "that which is stored up." Money represents the area of our lives that is most synonymous with our security. The love of money is called the "root of all evil" in the Bible (1 Timothy 6:10). Mammon is the golden demon that draws the poor into gaming halls and the rich into corporate takeovers, that fuels the Mafia and the madman. It infects the widow as she counts her mites, longing to have more. It numbs the miser who counts his shares of stock. This demon longs "to store up" enough to be really comfortable in old age. It causes the millionaire—when asked how much it would take to make him truly happy—to reply, "just a few more dollars."[2]

Baal, the golden bullock, or golden calf, in ancient Canaan was the symbol of many of those demonic forces we face in our spiritual warfare. The gold, of which the calf was made, represents the mammon. This money demon first entices us to have and then to have more and finally to have all. But the glistening bullock was also the symbol of sexual fulfillment. But representing money and sex were not all the golden bull represented. Baal was high and lifted up, an enticement to power. We shall deal in these three areas of our spiritual warfare: money, sex, and power.

Idolatry in the Bible is always symbolic of a kind of spiritual adultery. And all idols really represent the idolatry of ego. To have money is to have all and yet the Christ of the Apocalypse spoke sternly to the Church of Laodicea:

> You say, "I am rich; I have acquired wealth and do not need a thing." But you do not realize that you are wretched, pitiful, poor, blind and naked. I counsel you to buy from me gold refined in the fire, so you can become rich; and white clothes to wear, so you can cover your shameful nakedness. (Revelation 3:17–18)

Wealth is the demon that makes us comfortable with our own capability to provide from our own resources. Riches teach us self-sufficiency and wean us from our need of God. Money makes us believe that we have all we need to negotiate the rough times in our lives. Wealth therefore allows the demon, Mammon, to blind us to the possibilities of the surrendered life we can only know when we are willing to declare our poverty and reach out to Christ for completion.

It is rarely possible to learn to trust God for our complete deliverance in our time of need if we are convinced that money can make us self-sufficient. A group of lepers in 2 Kings are caught outside the city in a crossfire in a time of war. Having no choice about whether or not they will die of leprosy or be killed in the war, they are finally so hungry in a time of famine that they approach the camp of their enemies, the Syrians, to beg food. But when they get to the Syrian camp they find it deserted. The Syrians have fled. At first the outcasts see this camp as a personal storehouse for their own private wealth. They indulge themselves in riches. But after they begin to plunder the Syrian camp, they become repentant over their selfishness:

> The men who had leprosy reached the edge of the camp and entered one of the tents. They ate and drank,

and carried away silver, gold and clothes, and went off and hid them. They returned and entered another tent and took some things from it and hid them also.

Then they said to one another, "We're not doing right. This is a day of good news and we are keeping it to ourselves. If we wait until daylight, punishment will overtake us. Let's go at once and report this to the royal palace." (2 Kings 7:8–9)

These altruistic lepers, these eroded creatures from the tombs, teach us a simple wisdom: all we will hold in our cold, dead hand is what we have given away. The greatest wonder of grace is to find ourselves lepers in the midst of abundance. But nearly every time we stumble into wealth, we are usually motivated to think only of ourselves. The captivity of mammon is customary outside the church as well as within. Lured by the golden glint of mammon, the church trades its soul for goods. Affluent Christians find it difficult not to turn from Christ to worship the golden calf.

Money and the love of it are the number one temptation of many. Grace is really the province of saving lepers. But most contemporary lepers find their inheritance and keep it to themselves. And it isn't just grand affluence that spoils our reliance on God. There hides among the grand demons of affluence a host of smaller demons who wean us from the necessity of God. The sacred cows of the affluent may be the golden calf.

Of the three kinds of demons, this one is the easiest concealed by the church. Once when Jesus was teaching, a young ruler came to him asking the question, "What must I do to get eternal life?" Jesus reviewed for him the ten commandments. The young ruler confessed that all of these things he had done from his youth. Then

Jesus said, "If you want to be perfect, go, sell your possessions and give to the poor, and you will have treasure in heaven. Then come, follow me" (Matthew 19:21). It is difficult if not impossible to make this kind of statement about what we own. This was the rich ruler's real confession: "I own nothing and what I once owned, now owns me."

Remember, Satan's agenda is to own all those who will give themselves to him. So with riches, most of the transfer of ownership comes in little moments of giving our freedom willingly to his enslavement. Why do we do this? For three primary reasons. First we are convinced that money is the key to reputation. The second reason we do this is because we surrender to the myth that if we have more we'll be more secure. The third reason comes because of an equally widely celebrated myth, that if we have enough money we can buy anything.

The Demon of Reputation

> If I have put my trust in gold
>   or said to pure gold, "You are my security,"
> if I have rejoiced over my great wealth,
>   the fortune my hands had gained, . . .
> then these also would be sins to be judged,
>   for I would have been unfaithful to God
>   on high.
>
> JOB 31:24–25, 28

The gaming industry has gained a stranglehold on western culture, perhaps as never before. Lotteries and casinos are bigger than ever. They are cultural vampires that suck the poorer class of their last bits of bread and milk. As a pastor, I came to see those who trusted these demons living on vacant dreams. In many families I watched these greedy demons take the bread of the poor and leave their skinny children whimpering in the darkness.

But it is not just the easy-come allurement of casinos that dog the poor. Greed can be born among the disciplined poor too. I once had a college friend, who worked hard to start a little laundry. He took in old shirts and bleached and starched them into glistening newness. He labored night and day and did good work. Not only did his business grow but all that he touched seemed to flourish. Finally there were other segments to his business and to whatever he put his hand, there came profit and success. What began as a laundry, moved to real-estate speculation. As he matured into his middle years, his holdings multiplied, his speculations spiraled upwards, his stock options exploded. He became wealthy.

But as he climbed the ladder to success, he began to feel the necessity of being worshipped by every "underling" in his vast empire. What he first gained by honesty, he later gained anyway he could. The respect he longed for began to dwindle the more his wealth increased.

Even as his friend I could see that his values had slipped. He was swindling and stealing his way to the top of his empire, and I began to feel very sorry for him. One morning a farmer found his body in some shrubs at the end of a wheat field. He had been murdered, probably by someone in the Mafia, with whom he had made many deals. But the demon of greed was what really killed him. Mammon stood grinning over his foolish corpse in a lonely wheat field.

Satan tries to entice men and women down the golden road of material lust. Once we agree to love money supremely, we can no longer belong to Jesus whole-heartedly. Paul warned Timothy to steer clear of those who believed that godliness was the way to get ahead in the world.

> ... and constant friction between men of corrupt mind, who have been robbed of the truth and who think that godliness is a means to financial gain.
>
> But godliness with contentment is great gain. For we brought nothing into the world, and we take nothing out of it. But if we have food and clothing, we will be content with that. People who want to get rich fall into temptation and a trap and into many foolish and harmful desires that plunge men into ruin and destruction. For the love of money is a root of all kinds of evil. Some people, eager for money, have wandered from the faith and pierced themselves with many griefs. (1 Timothy 6:5–10)

Satan snares us with the idea that if we are rich enough we shall have reputation enough. Tevye in *Fiddler on the Roof* confesses musically that "when you're rich they think you really know." This is so true in the church that James wrote:

> Now listen, you rich people, weep and wail because of the misery that is coming upon you. Your wealth has rotted, and moths have eaten your clothes. Your gold and silver are corroded. Their corrosion will testify against you and eat your flesh like fire. You have hoarded wealth in the last days. Look! The wages you failed to pay the workmen who mowed your fields are crying out against you. The cries of the harvesters have reached the ears of the Lord Almighty. You have lived on earth in luxury and self-indulgence. You have fattened yourselves in the day of slaughter. (James 5:1–5)

Can it be the golden demons come even to the altar of the church? How sad that we who serve in the church are as susceptible to fraud as those outside it.

Paul reminds Timothy at the end of his first letter to offer this stern advice to the people of the church: "Command those who are rich in this present world not to be arrogant nor to put their hope in wealth, which is so uncertain, but to put their hope in God, who richly provides us with everything for our enjoyment. Command them to do good, to be rich in good deeds, and to be generous and willing to share" (1 Timothy 6:17–18).

"The rich would like us to give them the recognition they want but is so little good for them. They want us to give them adoration even as they tempt us to abandon the verities of eternity. Money has demonically usurped the role in modern society which the Holy Spirit is to have in the church," wrote Thomas Merton.[3] The demonic influence of money is what Richard Foster calls the "dark side of money" in his book *Money, Sex and Power*. Martin Luther would no doubt have agreed with Foster, for Luther spoke of those imperative, three conversions: the heart, the mind, and the purse.[4] What does Foster mean when he speaks of the dark side of money?

> I am referring both to the way in which money can be a threat to our relationship with God and to the radical criticism of wealth that we find so much of in Jesus' words. The warnings and exhortations are repetitious, almost monotonous. "Woe to you that are rich" (Luke 6:24). "You cannot serve God and mammon" (Luke 16:13). "Do not lay up for yourselves treasure on earth" (Matthew 6:19). "It is easier for a camel to go through the eye of a needle than for a rich man to enter the kingdom of God" (Matthew 19:24). "Take heed

and beware of all covetousness" (Luke 12:15). "Sell your possessions and give alms" (Luke 12:33). "Give to everyone who begs from you, of him who takes away your goods do not ask them again" (Luke 6:30).[5]

Foster goes on to say that the demon that infuses our preoccupation with money is the demon of fear. We fear insecurity. We fear an inadequately funded retirement. We fear the loss of status or a country-club membership. We fear insolvency in the marketplace, bankruptcy, long hospital stays that will drain our years of savings into the coffers of the medical expenses.[6]

Is the terror real? Karl Menninger asked one of his more wealthy patients, "Whatever are you going to do with all that money?"

His client replied, "Oh, just worry about it I suppose!"

"Well," asked Dr. Menninger, "Do you get that much pleasure out of worrying about it?"

"No," said the client, "But I have such feelings of terror when I think of giving some of it to somebody."[7]

Here then is the terror that stalks us. The fear demon sews up our years in the fear of loss and the utter fear that we won't get our fair share. This feeling begins when we are young. Foster confesses that as a boy he was good at playing marbles:

> I could play marbles better than any other kid in the school. Since we always played for "keeps," I could often wipe out another boy's fortune before the noon recess was over. On one occasion I remember taking a huge sack of marbles, throwing them one by one into a muddy drainage ditch, and watching with delight as the other boys scrambled to find them. Through that single experience I began to sense something of the

power wealth can give and the manipulative ends to which it can be put.[8]

There is often a demonic joy in knowing we hold the cards and thus have the power to control or embarrass those who are indebted to us.

Jesus used particularly graphic parables to keeps us from the demons of money and the fear with which they strangle our community relationships. Consider the story of the unjust steward:

> The kingdom of God is like a king who decides to square accounts with his servants. As he got under-way, one servant was brought before him who had run up a debt of a hundred thousand dollars. He couldn't pay up, so the king ordered the man, along with his wife, children and goods to be auctioned off at the slave market.
>
> The poor wretch threw himself at the king's feet and begged, "Give me a chance and I'll pay it all back." Touched by his plea, the king let him off, erasing the debt.
>
> The servant was no sooner out of the room when he came upon one of his fellow servants who owed him ten dollars. He seized him by the throat and demanded, "Pay up, now!"
>
> The poor wretch threw himself down and begged, "Give me a chance and I'll pay it all back." But he wouldn't do it. He had him arrested and put in jail till the debt was paid. When the other servants saw this going on, and brought a detailed report to the king.
>
> The king summoned the man and said, 'You evil servant! I forgave your entire debt when you begged me for mercy. Shouldn't you be compelled to be merciful to your fellow servant who asked for mercy? The king was furious and put the screws to the man until he

101

paid back his entire debt. (Matthew 18:23–34, *The Message*)

Money is so often seen as the key to our security and reputation. Wise are those who recognize it's snares.

The Demon of Leisure

Then he told them this story: "The farm of a certain rich man produced a terrific crop. He talked to himself: 'What can I do? My barn isn't big enough for this harvest.' Then he said, 'Here's what I'll do; I'll tear down my barns and build bigger ones. Then I'll gather all my grain and goods and say to myself, "Self, you've done well! You've got it made and can now retire. Take it easy and have the time of your life!" ' Just then God showed up and said, 'Fool! Tonight you die!'"

LUKE 12:16–20 *THE MESSAGE*

Money gratifies the ego by buying us leisure. Most of us long to be able to thumb our nose at our employer and declare ourselves free of the workplace forever. Too often we act as though both our time and money are ours to spend as we wish.

Most people who spend their lives looking forward to leisure wind up dying within a relatively short time after they achieve their goal. Though they knew how to esteem leisure, they never carried the proper esteem for their work. Most who finally do achieve leisure are forced to admit they are dogged by feelings of unrelatedness and insignificance. Too late they discover that nothing is quite so rewarding as the faithful execution of what they feel they were born to do. None are quite so happy as those whose lives are plugged into that special matrix of meaning that tells them they matter because they offer something valuable to others.

God is the one who calls us and gives meaning to our lives. When God is in a life, it becomes meaningful and always has an answer to the question "Why am I here?" Satan, on the other hand, is the god of leisure. He causes people to become trapped in ego and the never-ending quest for time off. Those who follow Satan pursue an elusive idea of freedom. Yet in the misery of being undefined and without purpose, they may become suicidal or hypochondriac.

A man in one of Jesus' parables seeks only freedom. The answer to his hassled life, as he sees it, is to build bigger barns. By generously furnishing his future, he can truly take it easy. But does he want to take it easy so he can find some great purpose for which to dedicate the rest of his life? Of course not. He wants to be free for the sake of being free. But this is the worst slavery of all for it is the slavery of indulgence. The very day his retirement begins, his soul is required. And as he moves toward the grave, the only sound to be heard is the slightly perceptible laughter of demons. His ego was not served. His freedom was not achieved. But his grave was, I suppose, a kind of leisure. Death, after all is as reasonable as living for oneself. Neither produces anything good for the world around us.

The Demon of "Everything's Got a Price!"

When Simon saw that the apostles by merely laying on hands conferred the Spirit, he pulled out his money, excited, and said, "Sell me your secret! Show me how you did that! How much do

you want? Name your price!" Peter said, "To hell
with your money! And you along with it! Why,
that's unthinkable—trying to buy God's gift!
You'll never be part of what God is doing by
striking bargains and offering bribes."

ACTS 8:18–20 *THE MESSAGE*

One of the wealthiest people I know faced a time
when his wife was stricken with an incurable malignancy.
He confessed he had spent years becoming financially
independent. His fortunes amassed in stocks and bonds
were suddenly too little to do him any real good. He had
to confess like so many, "What I wanted most in life simply
wasn't for sale."

The poor, Jesus taught, are always better candidates
for the Kingdom of God than the rich. The poor have no
hope of security except Christ. The rich have been able
to buy so much they never really reckon with those things
that can't be bought. In the third temptation, Satan
showed Jesus all the kingdoms of the world and then said,
"All this will I give you, . . . if you will bow down and worship me" (Matthew 4:9). This is the temptation of those
demons who crook a beckoning finger from the top of
every slot machine. It is the last hope of the foolish fac-
tory worker who bets his baby's formula the black ace
comes up one more time.

So often, when payday dawns, I watch the poor line
up at the state lottery window at the local convenience
marts. From their dowdy dress and the old cars, I can tell
they have not driven to the lottery store alone. They have
been accompanied by the same old demons with the same
old lies: "This time you will win. Sure you're behind a
month on the house payment but when those lottery balls

pop up, you'll be able to pay all your debts easily, on your way to buying your new car. Then at last you can go back to the pawn shop and redeem your Grandmother's Cameo."

With such logic the poor are kept impoverished. With such false hope much of the world goes to bed hungry every night.

Once, when I served as a pastor, my secretary called me on the intercom to tell me I had a visitor. When she showed the woman into my office, I could tell that I was meeting someone abused by utter depravity. She had sold everything to try to keep her children alive, and she had sold herself into a thousand temporary sexual relationships, just to pay bills. But now she was at the end of her rope. She could not go much further.

When I asked what she wanted, she said *money,* of course. She wanted money to pay her rent so that she and her little ones would not become street people. The amount of rent money she needed was not exorbitant for she lived in a decimated tenement where the cost of her flat was well within our church's ability to pay. And so we gave her the money. I drove her back to her apartment. On the way, I couldn't help but study the last ravages of the demonic. Satan had well lived up to his Greek name, *Apollyon*. He indeed is the *destroyer* and had succeeded in taking what was once a confident woman and leaving her a human shell whose bargain hunting for morality and self-respect would seem to be nearly over.

But is it really ever over? No. She continued to live the same lie that was destroying both her and her family. If only she had a little more she would be able to go on a little longer. But "a little more" is never enough, and yet it is the lie that will not die. When Christ comes into the human heart, the lie *must* die. The ancient psalmist gave us a wonderful, money-free recipe for happiness: "Trust in the LORD and do good; dwell in the land and enjoy safe pasture. Delight yourself in the LORD and he will give you the desires of your heart" (Psalm 37:3–4). There is but one real adequacy. It lies beyond buying and spending. It lies beyond the demons' never-ending lie that all things can be purchased and everything will be all right if only we have a little more.

Ecclesiastes utters a melancholy heart-cry for meaning. If ever a man tried everything in search of happiness, it was the writer of this book. His hunger of heart was that which lay at the center of his riches. He wrote, "A feast is made for laughter, and wine makes life merry, but money is the answer for everything" (Ecclesiastes 10:19). He had bought various fleshly indulgences from a score of promising demons and was forced finally to lament that nothing worked and that all was vanity (Ecclesiastes 12:8). The word "vanity" with which he referred to life means "empty." And yet he seems so deluded as to believe that he could take his emptiness of soul and "spend" it full.

Let us look at two extremes: the miser and the spender. Some desire money not for the pleasure of storing it but for the sheer pleasure of spending it. It is difficult to say which of these pleasures is the most ungodly. Embedded in both is the temptation to keep it all for one's self. As such, the joy of spending money is as narcotic as the joy of saving it. The spender wants more and more money for the joy of buying everything that titillates the eye. The miser wants more and more money for the joy of counting it. But both miser and spender are owned.

The spender is often no stranger to debt, a prospect that freezes the blood of the miser. Debt is rationalized as "manageable" until it becomes completely unmanageable. In this "buy-now-pay-later" day of ours, credit cards become a way for us to spend against money we will get in the future. What an odd contradiction this is: as we spend future money, we lose the future. Life for spenders never crashes, it merely constricts, until all kinds of obscene results occur: divorce, insolvency, and fraudulent check writing.

What about misers? Actually, they're spenders too. The miser keeps the money against some supposed day of necessary spending. He often basks in the prospect of being able to spend lavishly though he never does. The joy of *someday* spending it always outweighs the thought of spending it *now*.

The Apostle John wrote of the problem of money when he encouraged the church to steer clear of the lust of the flesh, the lust of the eyes, and the pride of life:

> Love not the world, neither the things that are in the world. If any man love the world, the love of the Father is not in him. For all that is in the world, the lust of the flesh, and the lust of the eyes, and the pride of life, is not of the Father, but is of the world. And the world passeth away, and the lust thereof: but he that doeth the will of God abideth for ever. (1 John 2:15–17 KJV)

1 John 2:16 is so elusive. What do the terms "the lust of the flesh," "the lust of the eyes," and "the pride of life" really mean? John Wesley interpreted these elusive phrases in this way. The "lust of the flesh," Wesley believed were those pleasures in which we indulge our outward senses (taste, smell, or touch); in short, all of the appetites including gluttony and sexuality. The "lust of the eyes" refers

to the pleasure of beauty and the imagination: in short, aesthetics. The "pride of life" means anything from which we garner other peoples' admiration: clothing, position, homes, autos, and all things, material—in short, power.[9]

Perhaps these three things combine to form the demon of "Everything has a price tag." Of course, these are not sins in themselves. Our appetites must know some fulfillment or we will starve to death. But appetites that take control of our lives destroy us. The appetite of hunger, if left in charge, will deliver us to the scourge of obesity and premature death. The appetite of sex, if left unchecked, will create a planet of lust. The appetite for the beautiful, will lure us into mental states that are wanton. These appetites can become the demon of "everything-has-a-price," which has the power to destroy us.

Conclusion

When I sent you without purse, bag or sandals, did you lack anything?

LUKE 22:35

In winning the spiritual war with Satan's money-demons, I want to suggest three courses of action. The first course of action concerns a way to win over the miser demon. May I suggest, at least for those prone to hoard wealth, that you may need to develop a habit of lavish spending. I realize that the poor cannot always solve their miserly tendencies in the same way as the wealthy. But even the poor may need to practice lavish spending to some more meager levels of extravagance. For the poor are as prone as the wealthy to love their money. The poor would rather keep it as a form of material idolatry than to set themselves free of its control by using it up. Lavish spending is an automatic way to remind you of the nature of God himself. At what point in either creation or human redemption was God ever stingy? You have only to look at the world of nature to see that God never scrimps or cut corners. He never cuts corners when he spends himself in a trillion acre field of wildflowers or the massive sculpting of a thousand river canyons.

Let your eye view Calvary for a moment and you will see that God is also never stingy in how he redeems. His purse was emptied to the last bit of silver when the blood of Christ flowed for you. There is a glorious touch of hedonism in God. He is the Big Spender ever purchasing pleasure for himself and all his children. When I look at God I realize I am serving the Deity of extravagance. I therefore will not cut corners while I pass through his beautiful world en route to his eternal realm. As long as my eyes receive the light I want to raise my alleluias before canyons, caverns, clematis, chickadees, the choruses of caribou, and the clamorous cries of carillons on clear mornings.

I am reduced so often to what I call "Christian hedonism." I cannot help but pursue these pleasures that name themselves after God. And my heart is so overwhelmed by divine generosity that I want to buy things and fling them at the world and say, "See, this lavish nonconcern is the picture of my God." I didn't have to spend "my good money" to go to Spain; I could have saved it. But not to drive to the Sierras at sunset or see El Greco's Toledo at dawn, is one transgression I will not sin. And I know many people who would back away from such extravagance just to run their adding machines and smile down with pride on the totals. But it shall not be so with me. I will spend it all, and bless God with every purchase. I have no trouble at all now with the miser demons. They cower before my recklessness and have nothing to do with me.

Like Mary Magdalene, I dump out the nard that might feed the poor and only later do I remember Judas's rebuke. But then like Mary Magdalene, I see God's love as lavish business, and I want to dump on Jesus' feet everything I am and have. I know that in reality I do not have much, but I will not let its infernal littleness lay hold of me. I want to die with empty pockets, giving as God did. When he comes for me, I want no undumped flasks of nard stored up in some stingy corner of my life.

Second, I know that for Christians the money demons can be defeated by learning the system of tithing. Tithing is much in debate by Christians these days. It seems a legalistic, Old Testament proposition to some. It is true that there are not a great many mentions of it in the New Testament (although Jesus seems to commend it in Matthew 23:23). Still, it is an old, old practice. Abraham, three and a half millennia ago paid tithes to Melchizedek, the king of Salem (Genesis 14:18–20). The word *tithe* relates to the word *tenth,* as the word *quarter* relates to the word *fourth.* To tithe is to give ten percent to God.

Tithing can hardly be called lavish giving, but giving ten percent is the remembrance of God in our earning and our spending. The wonderful thing about tithing is that it breaks the hold that money has on us. We do not give to God as though our little gifts might bail the Almighty out of some cosmic scrape. With our earthly pittances we cannot furnish heaven. But in tithing we are doing two things. First, we never tithe but when we include God as the major player in our material realm. When we give, we acknowledge that we are but returning something to him who has furnished us with all things. The tithe reflects of our gratitude to him who is the provider, Jehovah-Jireh (Genesis 22:14) of all good things. We do not create our income on our own. Only by his provision is the loaf on our table. In tithing we remove ourselves from that central arrogance that says our bread is our business.

But there is a second and even more wonderful thing that tithing does. It breaks the thrall of the miser demon, that makes us want to hold on too tightly to that which we have. When we give the ten percent freely and willingly to God, it is our confession that we are still in charge of our money, it is not in charge of us. For if we refuse to give God this significant amount, we shall keep it all, and in keeping it all we learn first to love it more than we love God. Then, at last, we horde it, and thus destroy that quality of life that comes through spending it. Therefore, if you will not give this ten percent to God, give it to anyone you will. If you will not give it away, then burn it. Do anything but keep it, for in keeping it, the love of it will begin consuming you. And your adoration will at last be demonic. Satan will own you, for he will have taken charge of your soul under his dark green name—*money*.

There is a third way of winning over the money demons. It is abandonment. Here and there are those whom God leads to abandon all. It was said of those early disciples:

> All the believers were one in heart and mind. No one claimed that any of his possessions was his own, but they shared everything they had. With great power the apostles continued to testify to the resurrection of the Lord Jesus, and much grace was upon them all. There were no needy persons among them. For from time to

111

time those who owned lands or houses sold them, brought the money from the sales and put it at the apostles' feet, and it was distributed to anyone as he had need. (Acts 4:32–35)

This is a way to win over the material demons. Any of these three answers to the issue of spiritual warfare must be given back at last to God.

Still I am stuck on the beauty of God's lavish mercy. His is a free beneficence that ought to encourage us to be as he is. His benediction is upon all those who love him. For these who receive his love enable him to win over all of Satan's allurements. In him the miser and the spender are dissolved in wonder. These above all know that the very best things in life are not so much free as they are evidences of his joyous extravagance. If you want to defeat the money demons, you have but to come to his grand party. The door prize is eternal life. The banquet is grace. There we are too ashamed to horde or cherish any of our worthless holdings. There the rich see his wealth and learn earth's most redeeming truth: we are all poor. Yet look at the anthem the prophet has given us:

> Come, all you who are thirsty,
>   come to the waters;
> and you who have no money,
>   come, buy and eat!
> Come, buy wine and milk
>   without money and without cost.
> Why spend money on what is not bread,
>   and your labor on what does not satisfy?
> Listen, listen to me, and eat what is good,
>   and your soul will delight in the richest of fare.
>
> ISAIAH 55:1–2

Demons rarely come to us in the lavish providence of God. In the extravagance of holy grace, the light is too intense for them. The same lavish light that frightens demons illumines our own bogus admiration of those things we once valued before we reached the far pavilions of God. But in this far camp there are no golden calves. There are no boutiques where you may buy. There are no banks where you can save. There is only your Father, who having cast out Satan, made a place for universal abundance. You must, of course, check your bank bags at the door. This requirement is not to reduce you to poverty but to prepare you to receive the only wealth that endures forever. Satan will trouble you no more once you have seen the true nature of wealth. Should you ever lose this wealth, you will have to look in the dim corners of the universe where human currency is still god. *Money* is a word strangely absent from the lexicon of heaven.

5

ASTARTE: THE DEMON
OF ILLICIT SEXUALITY

*Set your minds on things above, not on earthly
things. For you died, and your life is now hidden
with Christ in God. When Christ, who is your life,
appears, then you also will appear with him in
glory.*

*Put to death, therefore, whatever belongs to
your earthly nature: sexual immorality, impurity,
lust, evil desires and greed, which is idolatry.*

COLOSSIANS 3:2–5

*You shall not covet your neighbor's house. You shall
not covet your neighbor's wife . . .*

EXODUS 20:17

exual temptation may be the bulwark of Satan's most
frequent attack on our lives. To take up arms in this arena
of struggle requires constant vigilance. Our world is filled
with needless incentives to constantly stir our sexual
appetites. Billboards, television, movies, novels, maga-
zines, and radio use sex to sell products. In such a world
of instant fantasy, Satan always has a corridor into the
sanctity of our value systems.

As the symbol at the center of this chapter I want
to place Astarte. She has ruled from century to century
as the goddess of seduction. Her role and name change

only slightly from culture to culture. As Astarte, she was born in the Canaanite religions of biblical times. She is Ishtar among other ancient peoples. She is Oeastre in Celtic cults of ancient England. She is Artemis, the voluptuous goddess of Ephesus. She is Diana of the Chase to the Romans. She is the one who—from religion to religion—had temples of worship that included rituals of "holy" fornication and adorations of adultery acted out in her honor. In recent Western culture, Astarte is goddess to the cult of the "pin-up." She is the poster girl that American GIs carried in their wallets and fighter pilots painted on the noses of their airplanes. She lives from novel to novel and movie to movie as that omni-available source of fantasy and indulgence.

In terms of enticement and cultural image, Astarte is female. Her image remains primarily female from culture to culture and era to era. But the issue of sexual indulgence in our own time applies to both genders. Men more and more have become the politically correct "pin-ups" of a culture bent on playing fair with gender. Ancient peoples became obsessed with the sexual escapades of gods and goddesses and they nearly always came in pairs. Baal—which we will learn about in the final chapter—was the husband god. And in the book of Exodus, it is around this massive and masculine golden bullock that the children of Israel gathered around to adore, when they ate and drank and "rose up to play" (Exodus 32:6 KJV).

So while Astarte, the female seductress goddess, is the primary image of sexuality throughout the ages, the more masculine images of bulls, satyrs, and rapacious beasts of one kind or another are always secondary images of sexual temptation and indulgence.

But why talk of gods and goddesses in modern times?

More and more the enticements are contrived to please women in the culture. Lust has become the aggressive female. Any number of recent movies show the tempter not as Astarte, but Baal, the husband: *Fatal Attraction, The Bridges of Madison County.* The goddess Diana is now Ares, the macho war god, the super male who is the golden bullock of wanton feminine pursuit.

And what of Astarte? She is now more than the mere ultra-feminine symbol. In this libertine culture, she is the goddess accessible—the goddess of bargain morality whose worship has never declined because of her over-saturation in the culture. The bull too is so commonly worshipped there is not space to build all the temples his adoration requires. What Baal and Astarte sell is so "red-blooded and normal" that everyone has a right to it. It is no longer necessary to enshrine it at that special center of marriage. It belongs to all, whatever the sexual preference. Having lost its sacred status in the temple, sex has taken to the streets. There is a vulgar openness to human sexuality, which can be found in abundance in the tabloids and artifacts of adult book stores. But not only there. It can also be found in the more serious manuals and intellectual art shops of well-lit shopping centers. There are books that serve the culture outlining every kind of sexual exchange and photographically telling the interested how to stalk their particular taste.

Christians who often have a more separate and lofty view of the high state of godly sexuality seem rarely to protest. Every church these days holds tales of members who pursued divorce and remarriage opportunities within their congregations. The contemporary church has out-Corinthed Corinth. Years ago, *Christianity Today* printed statistics indicating that as many as 6 percent of America's ministers have committed adultery while serving as pastor. Another 6 percent of ministers had committed some indiscretion for which they had "never got caught." A more recent survey says that as many as 37 percent of America's ministers and priests have committed some acts of illicit sexuality that were never discovered. Many colleagues and pastors I have known have fallen from their pedestals of community esteem, having been deceived by Astarte. If this is the state of the church how wide is this arena of deception? How shall we define the size of the Christian's battlefield?

Remember: one of the characteristics of Satan and his angels is that they have no home of their own except the Abyss. This legitimate home is apparently one they despise (Luke 8:31). They have not yet been permanently assigned to this everlasting prison house. In the interim they are homeless, and as vagabond spirits from the earth they beckon us with intolerable seductions. They prefer to be almost anywhere on earth rather than in hell, it would seem. In Mark 5:12 the demons who collectively call themselves "Legion" are about to be exorcised from the demoniac. They beg Jesus to send them into the swine, instead of back to hell. Their status is that of evil wanderers.

In Job as well, Satan confesses to his vagabond, neurotic roaming of the earth: "The Lord said to Satan, 'Where have you come from?' Satan answered the Lord, "From roaming through the earth and going back and forth in it" (Job 1:7). About this same spirit of wanderlust Peter wrote, "Be self-controlled and alert. Your enemy the devil prowls around like a roaring lion looking for someone to devour" (1 Peter 5:8). This restless and roaming spirit of the satanic kingdom is pictured as though Satan is a feral beast, wandering and licking his chops, set on our destruction.

The Vagabond Demon of Indulgence

Not long after that, the younger son got together all he had, set off for a distant country and there squandered his wealth in wild living....

When he came to his senses ... he got up and went to his father.

But while he was still a long way off, his father saw him and was filled with compassion for him; he ran to his son, threw his arms around him....

Meanwhile, the older son ... answered his father, "Look! All these years I've been slaving for you.... But when this son of yours who has squandered your property with prostitutes comes home, you kill the fattened calf for him!"

LUKE 15:13–30

I remember overhearing two businessmen talking in an airport lounge. The one was asking the other, "Do you think you are going to play this trip straight?"

The other said, "I dunno, maybe."

The first man jumped back into the conversation by saying, "Come on, Ned, who's to know?"

Then Ned agreed and their conversation turned elsewhere. But their dialogue still remains in my mind. Two moral vagabonds, a long way from home, were about to yield to Astarte, the alluring personification of the one who continually paces the earth, like a lion seeking whom he may devour.

Satan's allurement can draw us far afield from our usual service and make us feel that somewhere, out there,

118

far enough from home, no one will ever know. Somewhere, out there, we can enjoy sexual adventures with no hint of stain. What is concealed will forever remain hidden.

Satan's wandering, pacing lifestyle allures the prodigal in all of us. There is always this feeling that if we get far enough away, we can cheat and no one will ever know. The desert was ever the place of sin in the Bible. The desert, Sinai, represented Israel's transience, her season of sojourn. Out there beyond the borders of that country to which God would guide her, things seemed somehow more permissible than they might later be in that place to which God wanted to bring Israel.

First, while Moses tarried on the mountain, the children of Israel and Aaron took off their gold earrings and made a calf of gold and cried, "These are your gods, O Israel, who brought you up out of Egypt" (Exodus 32:4). And the children of Israel "got up to indulge in revelry" (vs. 6). In this unhallowed land of their wanderings, they experienced sensuality and excused it in their minds perhaps because they were not yet at that home to which God was bringing them.

Again, in Numbers 25, the Israelite men sinned with the Moabite women and God's anger was unleashed. There is something about home that from the beginning of time, men and women mark as sacred geography. But away from home, it would seem that everything that remains undiscovered is permissible. At least this is the deceiver's lie to the traveler.

Temptation comes to us no longer in the form of a golden bullock. It comes instead in the man in the Calvin Kline ads—dressed in jeans and wet shirts. He is the super-macho, mortar-firing Rambo, whose image is stapled in *Playgirl* magazine. And Astarte smiles at us through the hazy smoke of cocktail lounges, barely visible in the corners of bar rooms. She is the vagabond who meets us where we want to find her, in those moments where we may pass as she does, silent and on our way somewhere else. Satan is the near-miss affair of a corporate executive who actually plans a business getaway with his secretary.

How splendid is the moral excellence of those men or women who remember that what they permit themselves is not just a sin against family but also a sin against God. It was an honest David who, after committing adultery, confessed, "For I know my transgressions, and my sin is always before me. Against you, you only, have I sinned and done what is evil in your sight" (Psalms 51:3–4). In truth, the pull of family will not always be strong enough to enable us to withstand temptation. Joseph in Egypt should be the standard of every moral man. It was he who answered the adulterous enticements of Potiphar's wife by saying, "How then could I do such a wicked thing and sin against God?" (Genesis 39:9).

These wandering, vagabond, everything's-okay-away-from-home demons must not be answered just in terms of our families. They must be answered in terms of the final tribunal where each of us shall give account before God (Romans 14:12). Indeed we must all stand before the judgment seat of Christ (Romans 14:10). The warning of the Christ of Revelation to the Laodiceans was that they should seek from him holy garments of innocence and sexual sinlessness so that the shame of their nakedness would not appear (Revelation 3:18). Remember that Jesus said that "There is nothing concealed that will not be disclosed, or hidden that will not be made known. What you have said in the dark will be heard in the daylight, and what you have whispered in the ear in the inner rooms will be proclaimed from the roofs" (Luke 12:2–3).

The late Ray Stedman was something of a mentor to me during my years as a pastor. I never knew him closely enough during most of my pastoral service to tell him how much he meant to me. But from afar off, I admired him. On several occasions I even had the privilege of meeting him and getting to know him before he died. I revered him as such a saint that I saw him as a paragon of virtue beyond any real temptation. Once, near the end of his life, we were on the same program in Vancouver together. As he addressed a large crowd of pastors, he spoke of the collapsing morality of America's ministers. And then he shared a part of his testimony that I had never read in any of his books or heard on any of his tapes. He said, in words to this effect:

You may think from looking at this old white hair that I am just a harmless old man and "safe" from the perils of temptation. But, alas, it is not so. Like all of you, I have had temptations in my time. Through the sheer grace of God I have remained faithful to him and my family. It is no more of a triumph than any Christian wife has to expect of her husband or that any Christian congregation has the right to expect of their minister. I would *like* to tell you that the victory that I found over sexual temptation came from my utterly, Holy-Spirit filled life. What I *must* tell you is that I'm not really all that holy. I never yielded to temptation but my victory probably came because of Luke 12:2–3. I just kept hearing my Lord say, "Stedman, there is nothing covered that will not be revealed, nor hidden that will not be known. Whatever you have spoken in the dark will be heard in the light, and what you have spoken in the inner room will be proclaimed on the housetops." This sinister horror of our discovery should keep us living for Christ, even when his motivating love for us does not.

The power of Stedman's integrity is with me yet. I would like to live in such a way that I disappoint neither Christ nor my beloved family. I know that temptation does not always come to us when we have been made strong by prayer and Scripture study. It sometimes comes when we are far from Christ, isolated from our personal worship. In this remote spiritual state we can drift into a kind of Christian "doublethink." In this state we can practice a laissez-faire sexuality while claiming a deep love for Christ.

Christalyn was a business woman in an our congregation. She and Elliott had been married for seven years and had two beautiful children. She came to me for counseling and said, "I am going to leave Elliott. Three years ago on a corporate trip to Milwaukee, I met a man who loves me and tells me so in ways that Elliott has never done. I can't live without him. He is awesome in bed, a real lover. Pastor, you've seen Elliott, you know how overweight he is. Furthermore, he is so unaffectionate and cold in bed he hasn't met my sexual needs for years. But Pete is different, look a this!" She took a picture out of her wallet. Pete was incredibly handsome. "We've been sleeping together regularly. I can't stay away from Milwaukee. On my last business trip, we agreed to divorce our mates and marry each other as soon as we can. I can't live without him, nor he without me." Then she added, "Besides being a hunk, he's a devoted believer in Christ!"

Satan was having his way with Chrystalyn's sexual drive. She was drawn to him by powerful urges that she knew were wrong. Yet she had always been faithful to church and however unfaithful she was to Elliott, she seemed to feel a need to mention that however things might look, she was still committed to Christ. But it simply wasn't true.

The whole nation was shocked some years ago when a prominent California pastor became the shameful center of attention in the national press. Over a period of weeks he had been counseling a woman who was in the emotional throes of depression. She had come to his office every week for psychological therapy and as he listened to her problems, he could sense that she felt better after their times together. One particular week, she phoned, saying that she was too "weepy" to get out and wondered if the pastor would come by her house. Reluctantly he agreed to go counsel her there. When he arrived she met him inside and closed the door, and then collapsed into his embrace in tears. He began trying to console her, and she began to caress him and before long—desire being what it will—they were in bed together. Then someone stepped out of the closet and took their picture.

Realizing that he was now the focus of a blackmail ring, the pastor, dressed and left the apartment and went to the police. An arrest was made of those who had tried to blackmail him. The pastor must be admired for not letting the incident be hidden by payola. Nevertheless, his ministry was over. At his farewell party, the church came to offer him condolences, and there were many tears. It was hard not to admire the way he had handled the scam artists, but it was no longer possible for him to serve as pastor, because he had played host to the temptress.

He had met Astarte, struggled, and lost. The vagabond demons of sensuality had captured him for a few seconds and years of his lifetime were lost to caprice. Only hell felt good about that awful day. The first way to wage effective spiritual combat is to know the limits of our endurance. To avoid every appearance of evil is essential for those who want to stand. The problem with the California minister was not a set of choices that began when he got into the woman's apartment. The problem began when he agreed to go to the woman's apartment in the first place.

The Scriptures encourage us to avoid "all appearance of evil" (1 Thessalonians 5:22 KJV). Romans 12:9 tells us to abhor that which is evil. Jesus said, "If your right eye causes you to sin, gouge it out and throw it away" (Matthew 5:29). There is no safe course in compromise with evil. Satan twists our legitimate drives—those that are wholesome and proper within the marriage commitment—into something decadent. His consuming firestorms are measured in seconds of betrayal that spoil years of fidelity. When you resist the devil he will flee from you (James 4:7). In the wake of the tempter, Satan's one desire is to do away with your spouse's honor and your children's esteem for you. His burning passion is to destroy your home. Make no mistake about office flirtations or corporate flings. Do not think yourself safe in the foreign city where your company sends you. There above all the vagabond demons may rise against you. Even there—especially there—Satan may try to destroy you.

Elizabeth, an excellent soprano in our choir, once came to me to tell me that she had fallen in love with another man and planned to divorce her husband. Like Christalyn, she made it clear to me that "she felt God's leading in the new relationship." "God has made it clear to me," she went on, "that he wants me to divorce Timothy and marry Carlos. God's leading has been so clear in this matter. What do you think, Pastor?" she asked.

"I think 'Thou shalt not commit adultery.'" I replied.

"How dare you judge me when Jesus is leading me so clearly!" she shouted. "I'm leaving this church and joining another—where Christians don't judge each other."

She did indeed leave the church. I worked with Timothy and prayed with him that she would return. But Timothy's love alone was not what ultimately prevented her from marrying Carlos. It was her love for her children that ultimately caused her to confess that she had been pursuing her new lifestyle not out of adoration for Christ but because of her fascination with illicit sex.

One cannot fail to be touched by the story of Hosea. Remember how Hosea received this commandment from God: "Go, take to yourself an adulterous wife and children of unfaithfulness, because the land is guilty of the vilest adultery in departing from the LORD" (Hosea 1:2). From that point on, Gomer, Hosea's unfaithful wife, becomes a living parable of how God feels about spiritual unfaithfulness. She is a woman enslaved to her passions, so much so that the children she appears to sire by her husband really belong to one of her lovers (Hosea 1:9). The rest of the book is Hosea's entreaty to sexual fidelity: the metaphor of God's love for faithfulness is the weeping love of a husband. Hosea begs his children:

> "Rebuke your mother, rebuke her,
>   for she is not my wife,
>   and I am not her husband.
> Let her remove the adulterous look from her face
>   and the unfaithfulness from between her breasts.

125

> *Otherwise I will strip her naked*
> *and make her as bare as on the day she way born;*
> *I will make her like a desert,*
> *turn her into a parched land,*
> *and slay her with thirst.*
> *I will not show my love to her children,*
> *because they are the children of adultery.*
> *Their mother has been unfaithful*
> *and has conceived them in disgrace.*
> *She said, 'I will go after my lovers,*
> *who give me my food and my water,*
> *my wool and my linen, my oil and my drink.' ...*
> *I will punish her for the days*
> *she burned incense to the Baals;*
> *she decked herself with rings and jewelry,*
> *and went after her lovers,*
> *but me she forgot," declares the LORD.*
>
> HOSEA 2:2–5,13

Yet the glory of the story lies in Hosea's unwillingness to let his wife go. When her passion has spent itself, she falls on hard times and is ultimately sold into slavery. Hosea's heart is broken, and he buys her back for fifteen pieces of silver (Hosea 3:2). Then he exults that beyond her sexual indulgence she still is his: "I will betroth you to me forever" (Hosea 2:19). Such overwhelming, unconditional love by one Christian mate for his or her spouse is an evidence of powerful grace that forgives and welcomes the violator back into the wholeness of all they have violated.

One of my students came to me one day weeping. "My wife," he said "has supported me all the way through graduate school. But she told me this morning she has

126

been sleeping with another man when she is on business trips. I am shattered," he said. "She has enabled me to finish school debt-free. She has worked day and night and spent every dime she has made to pay my every debt. But now . . . this!" He stopped and buried his face in his hands and wept. When he had regained control, he went on, "Now she wants out of that illicit relationship and has begged me to forgive her."

"Will you do it?" I asked.

"Calvin," he said, "do you remember Hosea 2:19?" I took my Bible from my desk and turned to the passage. The joyous words stared up at me even as he repeated them through his tears, "I will betroth you to me forever." He showed me the words that he had claimed with his wife as God's special promise to both of them:

> *Come, let us return to the LORD.*
> *He has torn us to pieces*
> *but he will heal us; . . .*
> *He will come to us like the winter rains,*
> *like the spring rains that water the earth.*
>
> HOSEA 6:1, 3

How beautifully they had met their crisis in grace. They are still together, and whenever they come to mind I realize that the power of God is stronger than the power of Astarte.

The Sirens of Betrayal

> *One evening David got up from his bed and walked around on the roof of the palace. From the roof he saw a woman bathing. The woman was very beautiful.*
>
> 2 SAMUEL 11:2

Ulysses' sailors in Homer's *Odyssey* were lured onto the rocks by the Sirens, those exquisite temptresses who destroyed men's lives forever. Throughout history, Christians have realized that demons often play a role in sexual temptation. Though human sexuality is a wonderful gift of God, it is easily diverted by Satan to the demonic realm.

Closer to home C. Peter Wagner tells the story of Jim Gaines a church elder in Orlando who gathered some friends and began rebuking the demons across from a particular adult bookstore in Orlando.

> Two weeks later and a half-mile down the road at a combined meeting of several Orlando churches, Metro Life Church pastor, Danny Jones leads about 500 Christians in prayer for the city. Then they enter into spiritual warfare, denouncing the demonic spirits that blind the eyes of non-Christians in the city and pulling down the strongholds that rule over the region. Specifically they denounce the spirits that control the "adult entertainment" businesses that sell pornography. Within a month, the city's Metropolitan Bureau of Investigation has enough evidence to start legal proceedings that could close the adult bookstores. Within two months, owners of all seven adult bookstores in the greater Orlando area voluntarily shut their doors.[1]

Most of the time Satan's warfare on decency is not as dramatic as that which occurs in witches' covens and black masses. However, it is no less damaging simply because it works in more normative ways. Christians with a great degree of spiritual resolution may still be caught off guard by its swift recompense. They may actually fall away from effective discipleship and never see their compromises as a kind of warfare at all until it is too late.

A man of my acquaintance in Maine, held a job in a grocery store working in a particular store belonging to a national chain. This man, whom we shall call "Jim" worked in the meat department as a butcher's assistant throughout his late high-school and early college years. A particularly important woman—a member of the city council—whom we shall call "Laura" always did her shopping in that store. She always seemed "extra-friendly." Finally Jim began to get a fixation on her. Laura never did anything explicit to encourage his fantasizes, but they persisted. Laura herself seemed to Jim to be his "ideal woman," and he determined in his heart that if it were ever possible he would like to have her.

The years went by and Jim went off to college and earned a subsequent master's degree. He ultimately married—quite happily—and had children. Later he was transferred by his company back to that very town in Maine where he had grown up. He loved the community that he had known and so did his little family. A wonderful thing happened just as Jim moved his little family to Maine. He became converted to Christ. His wife, who had prayed long for his conversion, was ecstatic. She had prayed so long for him that his conversion seemed worthy of a special dinner, which she prepared for him. They ate the dinner and settled down in front of the fireplace and were enjoying an after-dinner cup of cappuccino. Jim somehow felt free enough to tell her all his heart and so he did. He told her of Laura and his long-ago, adolescent dreams of having his way with her sexually. His wife smiled, and they read their Bible together, a newfound practice Jim began immediately after his conversion.

Strangely enough, the next day when Jim was driving into the hardware store, he noticed a blue Mercedes following his own car. The lights of the Mercedes began to blink. The driver was obviously signaling him to pull over. He did. He watched with fascination as a tall, willowy blonde got out of the Mercedes and walked up to his car. It was Laura, that long-ago centerpiece of his adolescent fantasies. More suddenly than he realized, his old longings were born anew.

"Jim," she said, "long time no see! My husband's gone for the week, why don't you follow me home. I'd like to fix you a drink and properly welcome you back to the old home town."

"Sounds good to me," Jim said.

In a moment he found himself following Laura up a long tree-lined driveway toward the huge home, a mansion really, where she and her husband lived. Her compulsions were obvious to him. Jim knew exactly where he was going and why he was going there. Yet he couldn't escape the grip of those long-ago allurements. His age-old fantasies were about to become a reality. He was contemplating how he would go about all that he had so long imagined, when suddenly, the image of his new-found Savior came strongly to his mind. He saw Jesus dying for him and the price he had paid. A huge battle was born in his heart. As a recent convert he suddenly learned of the power of his real enemy. It was not Laura. He was battling a spiritual power he had never recognized before.

Then he did something, he never believed himself capable of doing. He turned around and began driving the other way. Christ had won. But what really happened was that Jim discovered the whole arena of spiritual combat. It would not be the last time he would have to struggle with Satan. But God used a near miss to remind him that all Christians are involved in spiritual warfare. No one is exempt from this inner war. Every Christian has to learn that the conflict is so demanding that it cannot be won without the direct involvement of the Holy Spirit in our lives.

If you are a believing man or woman, you may already, in a weak moment, have given the devil some place in your life. Perhaps you are harboring some hidden Laura or some secret Jim. These illicit dreams may remain in spite of your marriage commitments to someone else.

I would remind you of two important principles in spiritual warfare. First, your body is the temple of the Holy Spirit. Paul reminds us that not only are our bodies temples, but we have been bought with the blood of Christ. When the conflict becomes extreme we must plead that blood and rely on that old victory already won by Jesus so long ago. Grapple these words to you with hooks of steel: "Do you not know that your body is a temple of the Holy Spirit. . . . You were bought at a price. Therefore honor God with your body" (1 Corinthians 6:19–20). The Holy Spirit has no temple in churches. Churches only contain him in the same direct proportion that the Christians who go there contain him. So we are his. He lives in us and does so because we have welcomed Christ, our Savior and Victor, into our lives. Christ who bought us and paid the price for us. So Paul is really encouraging us to see there is a double force here. We are temples built at enormous cost and paid for with exquisite suffering. We ought therefore to honor the Christ who lives in us. But it isn't just that Christ lives in us. He lives in us so continually that we cannot put him aside when we commit adultery or fornication. If we commit acts of illicit sex, the Christ in us is joined to any sin in which we indulge. He has taken up his inseparable residence in our lives: "Do you not know that your bodies are members of

131

Christ himself? Shall I then take the members of Christ and unite them with a prostitute? Never! ... Flee from sexual immorality" (1 Corinthians 6:15, 18). This then is the first principle of spiritual warfare, that we should not make a Holy Christ a part of personal immorality, for it wounds both him and our families whom we have married in oaths of loyalty and fidelity.

Once we have determined never to make the Holy Savior part of any infidelity, the second principle guaranteeing our moral safety is this: we must realize and remember who our enemy really is. We must realize that we can no longer afford hidden, quiet deals in which case we barter our souls for pottage.

> For though we live in the world, we do not wage war as the world does. The weapons we fight with are not the weapons of the world. On the contrary, they have divine power to demolish strongholds. We demolish arguments and every pretension that sets itself up against the knowledge of God, and we take captive every thought to make it obedient to Christ. (2 Corinthians 10:3–5)

After our inner love for Jesus, I suspect that home is the most warred-upon area of our lives. So much is at stake in our homes. And we must realize that if Satan can destroy that wonderful little womb of our glory and security, our effective lives are ruined. In a country where half of the marriages end in divorce, it looks as though Satan may already have most of the homes of America in his pocket. This is all the more reason to say that his spiritual strongholds can be beaten. The faithful believer remains determined that Satan shall not enter this sacred domain, for all has been purchased and indwelt by Jesus Christ.

The answer to controlling Satan in our lives is twofold. First we must be prepared to exorcise him in literal prayer. Wives must join their husbands in prayer that "Satan will be bound" from entering this inner sanctum of love and Christian living. We must not be ashamed to say it in just that way. Extreme temptation must be handled by the authority of Christ alone. While earlier in the book we talked about getting some anti-demon mantra that was all demonism. Christians do need to deal with evil by using the strong name of Jesus to deal with every satanic invasion.

A second strategy may be even more powerful than the first. Here you need no rituals of exorcism. You do not need to "bind Satan" to keep him out of your home life. Instead, begin a habit of daily discipline of prayer and trust. Those wives and husbands and young men and women who want to be pure before the Lord need only to walk in the Lord so consistently that his pleasure with our lives becomes an all-consuming drive. Then our love for him will express itself in such passion that we need not fear we shall betray him. The more you love your country, the less likely you are to become a traitor. The more you love your children, the less likely you are to become their abuser. The more passionately you love Christ, the more likely you are to live for him so closely that Satan will not be able to gain a foothold.

Conclusion

[My people] consult a wooden idol
and are answered by a stick of wood.
A spirit of prostitution leads them astray;
they are unfaithful to their God.

HOSEA 4:12

Sexuality is the issue of spiritual warfare that is always born in the idolatry of ego. It is not hard to see that most health clubs are surrounded by mirrors. For these mirrors become an instant playback mechanism for the admiration of those who are trying to tone and trim their bodies. But it is difficult to tell at times whether health clubs are more interested in preserving health or are they really temples to gender arrogance. One thing is sure, the demon Astarte rarely sleeps for long, and when she rises from her bed she is wanton and hungry. Those who are bent on union with Christ will have to reckon regularly with Astarte. Like other kinds of spiritual victory, the winning lies not in preparing ourselves for this desperate war but in living close to our commander-in-chief.

Idols have no affinity with the living God. Living in his presence is the surest way to keep the enemy at bay.

6

BEELZEBUB:
THE DEMON OF POWER

I will ascend to heaven;
I will raise my throne
   above the stars of God;
I will sit enthroned on the mount of assembly,
   on the utmost heights of the sacred mountain.
I will ascend above the tops of the clouds;
I will make myself like the Most High.

ISAIAH 14:13–14

Power is a major struggle for all believers. None of us is free from its lure. Perhaps any real look at spiritual warfare should start rather than end here. Power is not necessarily wrong. There is nothing wrong with the desire to be in charge. But the need to control can become self-destructive. It can define others as fodder for our own advancement and can turn those willing to serve it into bossy big brothers, corporate megalomaniacs, or banana-republic dictators.

The language of power, which runs throughout the Bible, is particularly strong in the New Testament. On every page one finds the terminology of power—those incumbents, offices, structures, roles institutions, ideologies, rituals, rules, agents, and spiritual influences by which power is established and exercised.[1]

Walter Wink points out that this all-pervasive language of power often appears as paired expressions in the New Testament. Not only does the word *devil* appear frequently in the New Testament, but if all the references to these paired words are considered as well, one can see just how much space is given to the kingdom of evil. These paired "power" words are everywhere: "principalities and powers" (*archai* and *exousiai*) appear ten times in the New Testament, twice by Paul and eight times by the Gospel writers. But consider these other paired expressions of power:

Rulers and high officials (Matthew 20:25),
Kings and those who exercise authority
  (Luke 22:25),
Chief priests and rulers (Luke 24:20),
Rulers and elders (Acts 4:8),
Angels and principalities (Romans 8:38 KJV),
Power and authority (Luke 9:1, Revelation 17:13).[2]

Paul even uses seven additional paired words connoting power not mentioned by the writers of the Gospels. Since the language of power pervades the New Testament, God must have more than a passing interest in the subject. Could it be because God understands that power is the highly sought force of ego and control? It can often be used humanely, but can also be twisted and perverted into savagery.

We Christians would never crave power openly. That might hurt our reputations for godliness. But we are awfully protective about our turf, and "turf" is just another word for personal empire. Turf is the way we retain our own throne while pretending to be free of self-service. The word *throne* (*thronos* in Greek) is used a 123 times in the Septuagint version of the Old Testament. The word is used 53 times in the New Testament, and while the word most often refers to God's throne it is used 3 times in terms of earthly rulers and 3 times to refer to Satan and his minions.[3]

But what are Christians to do with their own need to rule? How are they going to replace it with a hunger to serve? In terms of the Christian life, Christians are taught never to hunger after power and authority for their own selfish agendas. But we are to use wherever necessary our power over Satan. We have already looked at those passages (Luke 10:17, for instance) which examine the believer's authority over Satan. The power of triumphant living became ours at the moment Christ took up residence in our lives. When we became Christians, we did so by agreeing we would submit our need to control in our willingness to serve.

Often when you ask another Christian how they are doing they reply "all right under the circumstances." This particular cliché should never be a Christian's reply. Every Christian has been given the power to control his or her circumstances; we can indeed "do all things through Christ which strengtheneth me" (Philippians 4:13 KJV). But remember: Christians are only human beings. We sometimes allow circumstances to pile up on top of us. At such times we ought to be honest and admit that we really are "under the circumstance;" but we must not feel as though our failures should be covered over with a plastic platitude that confesses a false victory when we are really living in defeat.

Paul explains that our power for living honestly victorious is that very same power that raises dead Messiahs:

Therefore . . . I do not cease to give thanks for you . . . that the God of our Lord Jesus Christ, the Father of glory may give you the spirit of wisdom and . . . that you may know what is the hope of His calling . . . and what is the exceeding greatness of His power toward us who believe, according to the working of His mighty power which He worked in Christ when he raised Him from the dead and seated Him at the right hand in heavenly places, far above all principality and power and might and dominion, and every name that is named, not only in this age but also in that which is to come. And He put all things under His feet, and gave him to be head over all things to the church, which is His body, the fullness of Him who fills all in all. (Ephesians 1:15–22 NKJV)

Such is the promise of his power to all his followers. All things that threaten or frighten us are already beneath the feet of Christ. This immense power is ours by virtue of his victory. Indeed the whole satanic realm has been conquered.

While God's power is ours to use as both a weapon of advance and a wall of security, the strongest challenge of our warfare may be the lure to use power selfishly for our personal agenda. The temptation to have power was Satan's grand and final temptation of Christ in the wilderness. The devil transported Christ into realms of sweeping international fantasies and showed Jesus all the kingdoms of the world: "All this I will give you, . . . if you will bow down and worship me" (Matthew 4:9). This has been Satan's allurement to tyrants and emperors from Ghengis Khan to Adolf Hitler. Jesus recognized the lust for political power for what it was. He offered Satan the reply that worship belonged only to God. Worship takes us beyond our ego and reminds us who we are. In this remembrance we learn to subdue our power needs in order to bring our humanity into God's presence.

When tempted to power, Jesus said to Satan, "Away from me, Satan!" (Matthew 4:10). Jesus answered the devil with a stern no. Jesus did not equivocate: he would not own nations or people for the sheer joy of controlling them. Do these Scriptures seem a bit grand for your arena of life? Or are there places where you need to say, "Away from me, Satan!"? Could it be within the corporate structure, where you are tempted to sell your soul to please your overlords so you will one day occupy their chairs? Is it in your home where you enjoy controlling your husband or your children? Have you never realized that such addictive power-mongering is unlike Jesus who primarily calls his followers to be ministers and not managers?

Lets talk about the church. Churches are being destroyed every moment, because someone begins to believe they have the right to control. The Kingdom suffers from such arrogance. Self-importance, which will not bow at the cross and learn the important lesson of subservience, loves to manage and grins as it gains control of others. Pastors often leave a church because somehow self-important laypeople have come to prize control in the church, and the church bleeds because of such demonic power syndromes. The ghost of Ananias (Acts 5) still haunts the church with the demonic hunger for power. Do you not feel the plaintive cry of the Apostle who had been abused by such ungodliness? "Timothy, my son, I give you this instruction in keeping with the prophecies once made about you, so that by following them you may fight the good fight, holding on to faith and a good conscience. Some have rejected these and so have shipwrecked their faith. Among them are Hymenaeus and Alexander, whom I have handed over to Satan to be taught not to blaspheme" (1 Timothy 1:18–20). Paul has the same condemnation of the ungodly laypeople Hymenaeus and Philetus (2 Timothy 2:17) and Alexander "the metalworker" (2 Timothy 4:14) and Demas, the deserter, who "loved this world" (2 Timothy 4:9).

Power-hungry laypeople are yielding to Satan, and they are losing in this most critical area of spiritual warfare.

In my thirty-five years of pastoring I met all of Paul's ancient critics. Hymenaeus and Alexander, Philetus, and Demas were all part of my congregation at one time or another. The nights that I spent weeping over their carnality are many. None are so blind as those who will not see, and it has been my long-standing impression that those who are most in need of humility have so sold themselves to Satan's power temptation they cannot see the obvious nature of their control syndrome. They generally have the rhetoric of the church down well so that they speak humbly of Jesus, not realizing that they rarely talk to Jesus. They read the Bible but keep their reading so brief and fast-paced that the Bible cannot speak to them. They always pray, but publicly or in hurried formulas of table grace. They who are most shallow never realize they are shallow. The hurried, rote monotony of their religious habits bars their way to a real relationship in Christ.

I cannot speak for Paul's ancient enemies, but I suspect that they were "talking God" and "preaching humility" while they cut the heart out of real ministry. Hypocrisy is so much a part of religious power complexes that I suppose the two cannot be separated. The urge to control can go hand in hand with the urge to appear godly. Those who appear power hungry also need to believe themselves humble and selfless. I have often wondered if even Hitler believed himself to be acting out of love for the German people. I do know that most of those who brought injury to the church I served, usually felt both selfless and certain that Christ was directing them.

But laypeople are not the only ones whose longing for power destroys the church. As a pastor, so repelled by the this sins in others, I found myself sometimes prone to grasp after power for my own ends. I found myself having to beg Christ his forgiveness when I used my position as pastor to get my own way. I found this temptation so subtle that I would often find myself engulfed in corporate self-serving, before I realized I was acting out of self-interest while I tried to appear selfless. Are you a pastor or church staff person? You too may need to do a little inner personal inventory. Do not think that you are free of the warfare. Could it be in the church which pays your salary, you are struggling to be pastor of the largest church in the city? Of course, you would never say this out loud, lest you damage your contrived spiritual image. Have you lost touch with the Master? Where was such ungodly passion ever communicated by your Savior? Have you so mixed your desire to build a consumer-oriented church that you have forgotten that what people really want in a church may be less than God demands that his church be? Have you sold your soul to be the biggest or the best-known or the most contemporary? If so, you may have already struggled with the power temptation and lost. Let us turn our hearts to the measurement of these three allurements of power. They are all forms of idolatry: the idolatry of fame, position, and, for want of a better word, magic. With such simple tools, the demons drive wedges into the walls of our devotional lives. Through the fissures they create in these walls, they flood into our lives.

The Idolatry of Fame

Let nothing be done through selfish ambition or empty conceit.

PHILIPPIANS 2:3 (AUTHOR'S TRANSLATION)

The urge to be well-known is a piteous ambition unworthy of any who name themselves after Christ. Remember, he "did not consider equality with God something to be grasped" and indeed "made himself nothing" (Philippians 2:6–7). Fame can become the glitzy goal of the Christian life. Church soloists, organists, and dramatists can be motivated, just as those in the world are, by their need for approval and applause. An inordinate craving for fame can become as "neon" in the church as it ever is on a Broadway theater marquee. But somehow when Christians are driven by their hunger for fame, they are to be more pitied than Broadway actors. Most of the time this drive to be celebrated by a congregation only amounts to what Victoria Nelson called, in another context, "dinky fame."[4]

Winning over this demon in sequins is difficult for he settles in at the deepest levels of ego gratification. It was Jesus' second temptation. The devil took him to the highest pinnacle of the temple and there lured him with instant fame: "If you are the Son of God, . . . throw yourself down" (Matthew 4:6). Satan was really saying, "I offer you the shortcut of instant fame. When you land unhurt, you will be everywhere famous. It will be clear at once that you are the Son of God, without the necessity of Calvary." This theater demon now camps near the center of Christianity. Many churches have stage lighting and sound systems that rival that of concert halls. Many young people are captivated by the alluring performances of popular concert artists.

Within the church, budding young singers and "Christian entertainers" are no strangers to applause and performance. In dramatic style they deliver stirring solos to someone else's soundtracks that make the church a training ground for highly competitive young artists and preachers. There is nothing inherently wrong with singing, speaking, and "Christian comedy" delivered in a flamboyant and professional style. But shouldn't Christ's second temptation be allowed to instruct all those who want to succeed? Is there anything wrong with longing for just enough reputation "to get launched?" It is important for each of these young artists to remember that Jesus rejected the temptation to instant fame in favor of the costlier, slower way of the cross.

Perhaps you feel that I am being irreverent to suggest this new "yellow brick road" can be satanic. I admit it is suggesting more than I would really like to. But as Neil Postman has pointed out we live in the entertainment culture, and as his book title suggests we are in the process of *Amusing Ourselves to Death*. One can only wonder if the lure of Christian entertainment is not an evidence that servanthood Christianity is about to be swallowed up in the Jesus of "skotty-wotty-doo-doo-doo."

Malcolm Muggeridge wrote a wonderful essay called *The Fourth Temptation,* the thesis of which was that Jesus was not thrice tempted in the wilderness but four times. Satan's fourth and final allurement was to offer the Savior thirty minutes of prime time on network television. Muggeridge says that Jesus refused because faith is born in hearing, not seeing, the Gospel. Paul made this clear when he said, "Faith comes from hearing the message, and the message is heard through the word of Christ" (Romans 10:17). Perhaps Muggeridge was trying to say that Jesus rejected the lure of sensational TV fame for the same reason he rejected the lure of spectacular fame by leaping off the temple pinnacle.

Remember Shoeless Joe from Hannibal Mo? He was the star of *Damn Yankees* who sold his soul to the devil to get into major league baseball. While the Broadway musical was incredibly funny it suggests the same short cut to fame that pervades *Dr. Faustus* and any number of other literary works.

The church's addiction to entertainment is evident in the growing competition between mega-church stars on television. Production is as carefully thought through and presented as any documentary or Academy Awards night might be. When mega-church TV idols compete, is this all for Christ? Is Jesus even seen? Again Neil Postman counsels:

> Without ensnaring myself in a theological argument for which I am unprepared, I think it both fair and obvious to say that on television, God is a vague and subordinate character. Though his name is invoked repeatedly, the concreteness and persistence of the image of the preacher carries the clear message that it is he, not HE, who must be worshipped. I do not mean to imply that the preacher wishes it to be so; only that the power of the close-up televised face, in color, makes idolatry a continual hazard. Television is, after all, a form of graven imagery far more alluring than a golden calf.[5]

It would be splendid if all of Satan's good deals were as easily spotted as a six-foot seagull. Unfortunately, most short cuts to fame and recognition are more subtle. These shortcuts can take us unaware when we try to rationalize that we have no real interest in fame or power. Or these base desires take us captive when we say we are studying our competition to find out what to do to get ahead. In reality, each of these steps may provide deals with those smaller and not so obvious demons that lead us to mistreat competition or brutalize our way to the top.

Sadly, fame can become so overwhelming that it lures us to trade Christian humility for glitz and mere human applause. In such a trade everything beautiful is lost.

The Idolatry of Position

You said in your heart,
    "I will ascend into heaven...."
But you are brought down to the grave,
    to the depths of the pit.

ISAIAH 14:13A, 15

Not all power has to do with fame. There is another idolatry of power that has simply to do with control—controlling for the sheer joy of owning someone else's freedom. Such power has for its supreme appeal an ungodly premise that our own ascendancy is all that is really important. No one else matters in comparison to the great god ME! As it is in the church, so it can be on the job. One immense area of spiritual warfare can be our ungodly attempt to gain control of a corporation. Often we play by the same rules of power that are used to gain influence in the church. It can even be done with the same pretense of humility. The heart can reason deviously: "How can I gain more control in my company while appearing to be the servant to the entire corporation?"

Competition is never wrong in itself, but it can be the methodology of success. We begin our path to utter control in the idolatry of ego. Throughout the Bible, particularly the Old Testament, the shrine of ego is represented in the various gods and goddesses who competed. So often, as in the plagues of Egypt (Exodus 7–12), it is clear that Jehovah is challenging the pagan idols of the people. It is also true of Elijah on Mount Carmel; the prophet of God challenges Baal and his prophets to try and show Jehovah up in the matter of real fire. The prophets of Baal fail miserably, but the God of Elijah answers by fire (1 Kings 18:20–38).

Perhaps my favorite of all these stories of little gods challenging the only God comes in 1 Samuel, where the Philistines have captured the Ark of the Covenant:

> After the Philistines had captured the ark of God, they took it from Ebenezer to Ashdod. They carried the ark into Dagon's temple and set it beside Dagon. When the people of Ashdod rose early the next day, there was Dagon, fallen on his face on the ground before the ark of the LORD! They took Dagon and put him back in his place. But the following morning when they rose, there was Dagon, fallen on his face on the ground before the ark of the LORD! His head and hands had been broken off and were lying on the threshold; only his body remained. . . .
>
> The LORD's hand was heavy upon the people of Ashdod and its vicinity; he brought devastation upon them and afflicted them with tumors. (1 Samuel 5:1–4, 6)

Power like any other area of our warfare can be good or bad depending on what we do with it. If power becomes a weapon with which we dispatch those who are in our way to the top, then we invite the judging hand of God. But if power becomes that platform that we use to bless those who are waiting to gain or need to gain access to God then, of course, it can become a great blessing. Both Domitian and Constantine had great power. The former used it to slaughter Christians by the hundreds of thousands. The latter used it to make Christianity legal.

It is hard not to admire a William Gladstone who used his power to protect the poor and the abused in England. It is hard not to admire Mahatma Ghandi or Martin Luther King or Dag Hammarskjöld for using their incredible political clout to better the human plight upon the earth. It is easy to adore Jesus who, knowing all the power of heaven, only used his power to heal and save and resurrect the dead.

Once again, allow me to use Isaiah 14 to illustrate the horrors of abusive power. In verses 13–14, Lucifer demonstrates his own self-will five times. These are often called "the five I wills" of Satan (italics mine):

> *You said in your heart,*
>   *"I will ascend into heaven;*
> I will raise my throne*
>   *above the stars of God;*
> I will sit enthroned on the mount of the assembly,*
>   *on the utmost heights of the sacred mountain.*
> I will ascend above the tops of the clouds;*
>   *I will make myself like the Most High."*

Self-will issues from the lowest of all possible altars, the idolatry of the self. An old professor of mine, on graduation day, spoke to me of the dangers of self-will when he said to me: "I have no doubt that you will succeed," he said, "I just wonder what you will be when you have."

It was a cryptic parting word, but its wisdom has guided me across two score years. I have seen enough of the perils of position to make me afraid to barter with the demons of power for anything.

It is better to have nothing to do with Satan. This does not mean you must retreat from him in fear. Quite to the contrary, you must be able to stand up to him. In the name of Jesus he is subject to God's authority, and he cannot stand before the believer who is steeped in the spiritual disciplines and unafraid of Satan. Julian of Norwich says you may even dare to laugh him out of your life. Just as Jesus scorned Satan and treated him as nothing so would he have us to do.[6]

The devil will come to you with a globe and offer it to you for just one tiny genuflection. You have but to bow the knee a little, and when you stand straight again you will be in business with an all-efficient business partner. Elmer Gantry, though a fictional character, did just that. Jimmy Swaggart, though nonfictional, did it. The great industries and controlling corporations of the world are often run by people who gave themselves to low demonic shrines. These people win in the interim but lose in the long-run.

The Power of Magic

Thou shalt not suffer a witch to live.

EXODUS 22:18 KJV

Magic is the illusion that we cling to when we are forced to abandoned all hope. And yet there is still the feeling that counting on magic is better than abandoning hope. This magic abounds in the occult allurements that bid us believe in their dark hope when faith in God seems to fail. How does magic work? It promises a way out of our problems when there is no way out. It thrives on simple superstition, promising a happy life to all who will obey the laws of broken mirrors, leaning ladders, and the crossing of black cats. There are those who would never take a lottery ticket with the number 13 anywhere in the sequence. Las Vegas is a place where superstition abounds and where the money flows. In this "Oz of instant fortune," many place bets only after they have been to their own private shrines of the occult. These superstitious gamblers never confess their magical trusts. Nonetheless they would do no gaming at all except when all of the factors surrounding the game—from horoscope to their old lucky shirt they always wear—are all in place. In a similar manner, across the continent from Las Vegas, serious business people on Wall Street would not exercise a stock option when their horoscope is out of alignment.

I grew up in semi-rural Oklahoma where people waited for the moon to be right to plant their crops and the almanac to confer its rural blessing on their practice. The equipment is now gargantuan and expensive; the amalgamated farmer plants thousands of acres. But deep down many of these "hi-tech" farmers still play by the same rules as their more primitive ancestors with wood-handled plows.

Just how seriously is astrology's stranglehold on Americans? Virtually no newspaper is printed without some counsel to those under every zodiacal sign. Consider the all-pervasive rules of this magic. The combination of planets (Venus through Pluto), luminaries (sun and moon), and the zodiacal signs allow for 432 possible combinations of circumstances. There are what are called twelve celestial houses, which result from slicing the heavenly sphere like one might slice a grapefruit and drawing great circles around the circumference gathered by the central meridian at the poles. Where two planets are side by side in the zodiac, they bear a favorable relationship to each other and are said to be in "conjunction." This of course implies favorable dealing between parties relating or doing business. Companies trying to do business while zodiacal signs of their CEOs are 180 degrees separate on the sphere would be called unwise. The planets are said to be in opposition. Business dealing between two such opposites would be highly unfavorable.[7]

There are all sorts of other ways to try to employ some form of magic that will "guarantee" our arrival at some plateau of power. For many it is more flattering to think that those horrible things that have happened to us are a result of demonic influence than to think they are in mere psychological trouble. It is far more exotic to think that our misery comes from cosmic forces than a mere complex. In *People of the Lie,* Scott Peck discusses a very successful man named George who believed that he had sold his soul to the devil. He actually was suffering from an obsessive-compulsive neurosis, but this sort of diagnosis had much less appeal than believing he was demon possessed. If in truth someone is demon possessed, he or she is not responsible for any weird behavior. The psychologically ill, on the other hand, have to get treatment. The demon possessed are involved in a model of treatment that excuses them for cosmic reasons and therefore is far more exotic:

> According to this model, humanity (and perhaps the entire universe) is locked in a titanic struggle between the forces of good and evil, between God and the devil.

The battleground of this struggle is the individual human soul. The entire meaning of human life revolves around the battle. The only question of ultimate significance is whether the individual soul will be won to God or won to the devil. By establishing through his pact a relationship with the devil, George had placed his soul in the greatest jeopardy known to man. It was clearly the critical point of his life. And possibly even the fate of all humanity turned upon his decision. Choirs of angels and armies of demons were watching him, hanging on every thought, praying for one outcome or the other.[8]

Naturally, it is a lot more exotic for people to believe that they have sold themselves to the devil than that they are emotionally sick. You lose a lot of cosmic significance when you fire your exorcist and hire a psychiatrist.

When Bishop Pike hired the medium, Arthur A. Ford, to contact his dead son, Jim, he began playing with the dark side of magic that may ultimately have cost him his life. Richard Woods was convinced that he played along the edge of the dark powers and ultimately "plunged over."[9] Those who seek some "magic route to power" are likely to play along the edges of the dark kingdom. Such kingdoms everywhere offer them an endless supply of these possibilities. Clint Nichols quotes the following advertisement that appeared in a popular tabloid:

I will cast a spell for you. I can cast a spell to make one love another, or cause a person to change his mind about a relationship, or bring two people together. I can do all these things because I have the combined powers of my mother who was a sorceress and my father, one of the most powerful warlocks who passed on his secrets to me moments before he moved on to a different world. My magical powers are beyond your imagination. I can cast a spell in your behalf regarding a relationship, your financial situation, future events, or whatever is important to you. I have the power and I use the power.[10]

The access to magic is ever there luring and tempting the people who really have never gotten over their fascination with magic. As civilized Westerners we may find it hard to believe that we are not many generations removed from our forbears who created in us a proclivity for believing in magic.

These vestiges of magic are so common it would be hard to add them all up during a single day of our existence. When we say "God bless you" after someone sneezes, we do it because our ancestors believed that when people sneeze, they sneezed out their souls and unless they said "God bless you," legions of demons would run back into their space that the sneeze left vacant. The words *hocus pocus* are a contradiction of *Hoc Corpus meus est*, or "this is my body." These words were the Latin words the priest said when he changed the communion elements into the actual body and blood of Christ. Not only that, but some Christians still eat fish on Friday because of an old church regulation. Freya was once goddess of the horse in northern Europe when Christian missionaries encountered that pagan culture. On Freya's day, the pagans sacrificed horses to the goddess and then feasted on the horse flesh. Christians were repulsed by the custom and refused to eat horse meat on *Freya's day*, or *Friday*. So they ate fish to show they would have no part of these pagan rituals and feasts.

"You little imp!" as a rebuke to mischievous children goes back to ancient times when parents believed that young children could be temporarily inhabited by imps who stole their normally angelic bearing and gave them another mien. Our very word *booger* is a reduction of the medieval word *Boggard*, a name for the graveyard demon. The significance of numbers in our culture (in terms of their magic powers) would fill a whole book all by itself. What is to be the ultimate assurance that we don't appeal to our long-developed magical nature? Let us examine the "how to" of our victory over all that might compromise our spiritual dependency on Christ.

Conclusion

> *The Spirit clearly says that in later times some*
> *will abandon the faith and follow deceiving*
> *spirits and things taught by demons.*
>
> 1 TIMOTHY 4:1

> *Dear friends, do not believe every spirit, but test*
> *the spirits to see whether they are from God. . . .*
> *Every spirit that acknowledges that Jesus Christ*
> *has come in the flesh is from God.*
>
> 1 JOHN 4:1–2

The problem of demonic control is indeed most subtle. Most of those who are truly evil have not been able to see their evil. "One of the most disturbing facts that came out in the Eichmann trial was that a psychiatrist examined him and pronounced him *perfectly sane*. We equate sanity with a sense of justice, with humanness, with prudence, with the capacity to love and understand other people."[11]

One of the most demonic men I have ever known saw himself as the loving father of nine children—all of whom were terrified of him. Not only were they terrified of him, but his large gun collection and his offhand, explosive manner left them terrified. I came to believe that he was as close to being demonic as a human being can be. Yet he never saw the evil that filtered through every area of his personality. "In the Third Reich the very idea of *volk*—race—became captive to the egomania of Aryan supremacy. Those who have seen the crematories of Dachau and Auschwitz do not find it hard to believe in the demonic powers," said Richard Foster.[12] None who have known evil bankers who smiled during foreclosures that have dispossessed the poor can hesitate to believe in the demonic nature of power.

Richard Foster offers five approaches to defeating the demonic temptations to power: First, we should recognize that Christ in his death and resurrection has already dealt a death blow to the powers (Colossians 2:15). Second, we learn the art of defeating the powers when we learn the art of discerning the powers (1 Corinthians 12:10). Third, we can take a stand against the powers when we face forthrightly those demons that are trying to take possession of our own lives; evil is a matter of importance to all, and none of us are safe from it. Fourth, says Foster, we defeat the claim of evil over our lives when we practice a life of renunciation; after all, so much of our desire to be people of power, is born out of our desire to have material things. Finally, we defeat powers by the simple resolution that we will not ever desire to own or control anyone else.[13]

Perhaps the key issue of defeating Satan in our lives is born in a simple twofold realization. After describing a couple of terrifying exorcisms in which he was involved, Scott Peck offers these two observations. First, human free will—the desire to be free of Satan's control—is most important.

Human free will is basic. It takes precedence over healing. Even God cannot heal a person who does not want to be healed. At the moment of expulsion both these patients voluntarily took the crucifix, held it to their chests and prayed for deliverance. Both chose that moments to cast their lots with God. Ultimately it is the patient himself or herself who is the exorcist.[14]

But Peck also concedes that at the moment of expulsion—that moment when the demon is driven out—God alone is the answer:

I cannot fully explain what happens in this moment, but I can state that the role of the exorcist in this moment is the least important. The desperate prayers of the team are more important. These prayers are for God or Christ to come to the rescue, and each time I had the sense that God did just that. As I said earlier, it is God that does the exorcising.[15]

The Greek word *palé* means *to stand,* which is used in Ephesians 6:11 and 14. The way to resist the devil is to "stand." I discussed the issue of standing in the early chapters of the book, it yet remains the Christian's best defense. To keep from being owned by the demons of power, it is a matter of naming the powers. For then we shall be armed with our love for Christ. He has already conquered our enemy, and armed with his love our enemy is forever vanquished.

The victory of Christ on the cross has guaranteed our temporal security. We are indwelt by the Spirit and overlaid by the armor. When the Christ who won at Calvary fills us, it is clear that we ourselves will win. But let us remember this: not only did Christ win over the devil at Calvary, he will also win the last war. Since Christ nailed

155

our defeat to the cross, "having wiped out the handwriting of requirements that was against us, which was contrary to us. And he has taken it out of the way, having nailed it to the cross. Having disarmed principalities and powers, He made a public spectacle of them, triumphing over them in it" (Colossians 2:14–15 NKJV).

Now the glory is that Christ's victory over the devil's control over us in the past is about to be joined by his coming victory over the devil himself. We live between his Cross victory and his final victory. In such a period of history, we can only know his enduring victory in all of the skirmishes or battles of our own spiritual warfare. We have seen his Cross victory. Let us consider the one that is yet to come.

> I saw heaven standing open and there before me was a white horse, whose rider is called Faithful and True. With justice he judges and makes war. His eyes are like blazing fire, and on his head are many crowns. He has a name written on him that no one knows but he himself. He is dressed in a robe dipped in blood, and his name is the Word of God. The armies of heaven were following him, riding on white horses and dressed in fine linen, white and clean. Out of his mouth comes a sharp sword with which to strike down the nations. "He will rule them with an iron scepter." He treads the winepress of the fury of the wrath of God Almighty. On his robe and on his thigh he has this name written: KING OF KINGS AND LORD OF LORDS. (Revelation 19:11–16)

NOTES

Chapter 1: Enemy Occupied Territory

1. John Dart, "Evangelicals, Charismatics Prepare for Spiritual Warfare," *Los Angeles Times* (17 February, 1990), F. 16. Quoted in John MacArthur, *How to Meet the Enemy* (Wheaton, Ill.: Victor, 1992), 8.

2. MacArthur, *How to Meet the Enemy*, 41.

3. MacArthur, *How to Meet the Enemy*, 42.

Chapter 2: The Fury of Angels

1. Walter Wink, *Naming the Powers* (Philadelphia: Fortress Press,), 110–111.

2. Wink, *Naming the Powers*, ix.

3. John P. Newport, *Demons, Demons, Demons* (Nashville: Broadman, 1972), 15–16.

4. William Peter Blatty, *The Exorcist* (New York: Harper & Row, 1971), v. Quoted in the frontispiece.

5. Paul Billheimer, *Destined for the Throne* (Fort Washington, Penn.: Christian Literature Crusade, 1975), 18.

6. George Mallone, *Arming for Spiritual Warfare* (Downers Grove, Ill.: InterVarsity Press, 1990), 44–45.

7. Mallone, *Arming for Spiritual Warfare*, 45.

8. MacArthur, *How to Meet the Enemy*, 156, 157.

9. MacArthur, *How to Meet the Enemy*, 91.

10. MacArthur, *How to Meet the Enemy*, 105.

11. Madame Guyon, *Madame Guyon* (Chicago: Moody Press, 1960), 243–44.

Chapter 3: The Rumor of Victory

1. M. Scott Peck, *People of the Lie* (New York: Simon and Schuster, 1983), 47–48.

2. Wink, *Naming the Powers*, 21–22.

3. Wink, *Naming the Powers*, 21–22.

4. Wink, *Naming the Powers*, 21–22.

5. Thomas B. White, *Engaging the Enemy*, C. Peter Wagner, ed. (Ventura, Calif.: Regal Books, 1991), 61–62.

6. Clint E. Arnold, *Ephesians, Power and Magic* (Grand Rapids, Mich.: Baker, 1989), 54.

7. Arnold, *Ephesians, Power and Magic*, 55.

8. Newport, *Demons, Demons, Demons*, 36, 47.

9. Koch, *ibid*, p. 26.

10. MacArthur, *How to Meet the Enemy*, 20–23.

11. MacArthur, *How to Meet the Enemy*.

Chapter 4: Mammon: The Money Demon

1. Brother Ugolino, *The Little Flowers*, 44–45, as quoted in Richard Foster, *Money, Sex and Power* (San Francisco: Harper & Row, 1985), 184–85.

2. Foster, *Money, Sex and Power*.

3. Foster, *Money, Sex and Power*, 19.

4. Foster, *Money, Sex and Power*.

5. Foster, *Money, Sex and Power*, 20–21.

6. Foster, *Money, Sex and Power*, 22.

7. Foster, *Money, Sex and Power*, 43.

8. Foster, *Money, Sex and Power*, 32.

9. E.M. Bounds, *Winning the Invisible War* (Springdale, Penn.: Whitaker House, 1894), 64–65.

Chapter 5: Astarte: The Demon of Illicit Sexuality

1. Wagner, *ibid*, 33.

Chapter 6: Beelzebub: The Demon of Power

1. Wink, *Naming the Powers,* 99.

2. Wink, *Naming the Powers,* 7.

3. Wink, *Naming the Powers,* 19.

4. Victoria Nelson, *On Writer's Block* (New York: Houghton Mifflin, 1993), 144.

5. Neil Postman, *Amusing Ourselves to Death* (New York: Penguin, 1985), 122–23.

6. Julian of Norwich, *Showings,* translated by James Walsh, S.J. (New York: Paulist, 1978), 187–89.

7. John Warwick Montgomery, *ibid.,* p. 108.

8. Peck, *People of the Lie,* 37–38.

9. Montgomery, *ibid,* 145.

10. Arnold, *Powers of Darkness, ibid.,* 13–14.

11. Peck, *People of the Lie,* 265.

12. Foster, *Money, Sex and Power,* 183.

13. Foster, *Money, Sex and Power,* 180–91.

14. Peck, *People of the Lie,* 197.

15. Peck, *People of the Lie,* 196.

Other Books in the Growing Deeper Series You Will Enjoy

Church: Why Bother? My Personal Pilgrimage
   by Philip Yancey

Water My Soul: Cultivating the Interior Life
   by Luci Shaw

Whole Prayer: Speaking and Listening to God
   by Walter Wangerin Jr.

*The Wisdom of Each Other: A Conversation Between
Spiritual Friends* by Eugene H. Peterson